RELEVAN†

Questions and Conversations on
Faith in the 21st Century

JEFF WIDENHOFER

MEDIA.COM

Jeff Widenhofer

ILLUMIFY MEDIA GLOBAL
Littleton, Colorado

RELEVANT

Published by
Illumify Media Global
www.IllumifyMedia.com
"Let's bring your book to life!"

Library of Congress Control Number: 2021900499

Paperback ISBN: 978-1-947360-82-2
eBook ISBN: 978-1-947360-83-9

Typeset by Jennifer Clark
Cover design by Debbie Lewis

Printed in the United States of America

To everyone with whom I ever had a meaningful discussion on life and faith.

"Therefore, I am not yet discouraged about the future. Granted that the easy-going optimism of yesterday is impossible. Granted that we face a world crisis which leaves us standing so often amid the surging murmur of life's restless sea. But every crisis has both its dangers and opportunities. It can spell either salvation or doom. In a dark, confused world the Kingdom of God may yet reign in the hearts of men."

—Dr. Martin Luther King, Jr., the closing words of his book *Strength to Love*

CONTENTS

INTRODUCTION
A NEW DISCUSSION

This book is for anyone who wants a new discussion on faith in the twenty-first century. It's for Christians, ex-Christians, church members, former churchgoers, and anyone else who thinks this kind of discussion is needed today.

So much has changed. Even before a worldwide pandemic upended everything, new questions were emerging about how we live. What does it mean to live well? How do we live with beauty, depth, and meaning in our shallow culture? And today profound questions are facing collective Christianity. What does it mean to have faith today? What role does it play in our lives? Does it change anything? Does it help us live better?

Millions of people have left the church over the past two decades. Their rate of departure was steady, and it's safe to say that millions more will follow. Why has this happened? Why don't these people come back amidst economic hardship, sickness, high divorce rates, political turmoil, wars, neighborhood violence, social injustice, mental health problems, and a host of other challenges facing us today? What does this say about the message of the church?

There is so much longing in our culture today. I'm not talking about the longing for more material goods, wealth, or social status. I'm talking about fulfillment, purpose, and meaning. The good stuff. The really deep and important stuff. We want these things in our work, our relationships, and our communities. But so often we don't have them.

We want more out of life. We want to *feel* more and we want to *be* more. We want to rise out of the pervasive emptiness that seems to plague our culture today. We want to feel more connected. We want to feel like we can make an impact. And we want to feel something bigger than ourselves. But so often we don't. That's because it's not easy to do today. Our culture often stops short of delivering anything meaningful or lasting. It struggles to give us much of anything that has depth. And although the Christian church has traditionally tried to help people transcend their culture's shortcomings, for many people today, it doesn't. The message that the church preaches has become unimportant and irrelevant to vast numbers of people. We know this because studies show that church attendance has been on a steady decline this century. Millions of people have left the church and there's no sign of that trend changing.

Interest in living well, however, is now deeply important to our population, so much so that it spawned a booming business of self-improvement books, podcasts, programs, retreats, and seminars. It also brought about widespread interest in mindfulness, self-aware-ness, and psychotherapy. And for many people, even those who don't attend church, their belief in God is still real. It still matters. Or at least it could matter, if it had any place in their lives. But for so many people, it doesn't. The version of faith that many churches practice is abstract and absent from the daily grind of the twenty-first century. Many people are taught that their faith is mostly about holding onto the *right* beliefs, bowing down in worship, and securing a ticket to some exclusive post-death paradise. And that just doesn't relate to anything happening in their lives. It's neither relevant nor meaning-ful, so people find better things to do with their time than entertain this kind of faith.

Today it's time to consider how our faith can help us live better. It's time to talk about how it can reach into every corner of our lives, into every moment, into our relationships and communities, and how it can transform our lives into something more beautiful, impactful, and profound. It's time to talk about how our faith can be relevant. This is what I needed. After spending my entire life in the church and then leaving it without any regrets, I found something so much bigger and so much more important than what I was often given in church. And it's grounded in a way of life that the man at the center of the Christian religion promoted two thousand years ago.

This man spent his life teaching people about how their faith could help them live better. He showed people how they could feel fulfilled, and how they could have purpose. His message was an instruction on how they could experience an awesome and uplifting kind of life, one that was filled with beauty and depth, all the stuff that we long for today. And he wanted them to think big! He talked constantly about mind-sets that rise above the pettiness of culture, behaviors that move beyond what religious leaders were displaying, and approaches to living that really do result in good things. He called these good things "fruit." The kind of life that seeks these things is what he called an "eternal" kind of life. It's a life grounded in selflessness and love. It moves in a kind of union with God, and it's in tune with the expansiveness of God.

Christians often assume that "eternal life" happens after they die, but the man at the center of the Christian religion spoke about it in the present tense. He said we can have it now. He said that some people already had it, that those people were choosing to "walk in the light" and to live in "heaven." But others, like the religious leaders of his time, refused to have it. Those people grounded their lives in self-centeredness and self-importance. And as each of us understands today, this kind of life can have terrible consequences. It can lead to emptiness, no matter how much earthly wealth, popularity, or success we attain. It sounds a lot like all those awful depictions of hell: tortuous, unsatisfying, and disconnected. And in our own culture of self-centeredness and self-importance, we don't have to look far to notice that vast numbers of people are experiencing this kind of life. In fact, I suspect that each of us has experienced it.

Despite what many of us hear from the church—that faith is about abstract beliefs, worship events, and death—the message and example that Jesus gave us was ultimately about life. It was about the manner in which we live and what we will experience when we ground our lives in good things: love, humility, generosity, and self-lessness. And that could be a game changer for a lot of people today. It could offer so much more for people who are looking for a better way to live. This kind of life, the *way* of Jesus Christ, really could be a profound answer for us as individuals and as a culture. It could be a solution to so much of the ugliness, smallness, and darkness that we experience in our lives—all the things that we want to move beyond.

As you read through this book, think about life. Your life. Today. Right now. Think about what it is and what it could be. And don't think small. Don't think that a few scholarly conclusions about abstract spiritual concepts will resolve it. This belief-in-God stuff can be so much bigger than worship services, Bible readings, and assumptions about the afterlife. It can be so much more than just that. It really can reach into your life and transform it into something beautiful, impactful, and profound.

———

I want to be very clear. This book does not intend to answer every-one's important spiritual, theological, or existential questions. Perhaps more than answers, this book is about questions. From what I can tell, neither our culture nor our religious institutions ask enough important questions today. Most of the time they just prefer to double down on their version of the solution to everything. So today we must work to identify and articulate our questions, doubts, and uncertainties. We must unabashedly acknowledge them and face them, like we would with a therapist when we uncover truths for our lives. We must give words to them and name them. Because when we identify them, they take form in front of us. And only then can we see a path beyond them.

Neither will this book promote religion, the practice of our collective spiritual beliefs. There are more versions of the Christian religion out there than you could ever sample. So feel free to do that, but remember that God didn't create the Catholic religion, the Orthodox church, or any Protestant denomination. Humans did. And God doesn't need an established religion to reach us. The Christian religion could be wiped from the face of the earth along with every copy of the Bible, and God would remain. And humans would still have goodness written on our hearts, just like the Bible states so many times. And we could still connect with God.

Nor is this book about doctrine, the codifying of our collective thoughts on theology. For centuries the Christian church has practically made a religion out of publishing doctrine. That's why there exists a wide variety of distinct Christian sects and denominations today. They all come from people with unique perspectives. Reverend Wil Gafney, a Bible scholar and seminary professor, stated that the Bible is always interpreted through the "lenses or intellectual postures" of the reader. She reminds us that every individual and every culture creates theology from its own unique perspective. So when anyone, no matter their clerical position or level of education, reads the Bible and declares that a passage means something, "that is an act of interpretation."[1] Humans cannot escape this reality. So which doctrinal system is *right*? Who's to say? That's up to each individual to decide.

Nor is this book just about beliefs. Christians can get so worked up over their spiritual and theological beliefs, and they can experience a great deal of anxiety over other people's beliefs. There will never be one perfect set of spiritual and theological beliefs that all humans will embrace, even with the Bible as the primary source. So at what point do we move beyond our concern over beliefs? At what point do we move beyond debates over abstract spiritual convictions and move to embody goodness and good *fruit*? Spiritual and theological beliefs are not unimportant, but no human could ever design an effective comprehensive system of spiritual belief for all of humanity. And that's awesome, because it reveals the importance of *choice*.

This book is absolutely about choice. When we were created, each of us was given the freedom to handle important matters and answer important questions however we choose. This freedom is a gift from God. Unfortunately, choice often gets shoved into a corner when religious leaders become overly preoccupied with rules, expectations, and authoritative conclusions on Scripture. That works fine as long as people subscribe to their rules, expectations, and conclusions. But sometimes people unsubscribe. And if you haven't noticed, a whole lot of people have been unsubscribing lately. Millions of people, in fact. Surveys, statistics, and trends tell us so. So it's time to talk about the importance of choice in matters of our faith.

This book is also about discussion. Unfortunately, we are rarely encouraged to start new discussions today. Commercial entities work to control narratives rather than foster open dialogues about what matters to us. And most churches are reluctant to encourage people to think for themselves. Institutional religion prefers to hold its discussions within set boundaries of established norms and conventions, and so they rarely promote our God-given freedom to form our own opinions. It's interesting that the man at the center of the Christian religion was constantly asking people what they thought. He was constantly asking people what they believed. And he didn't seem to be looking for "correct," textbook answers. He seemed to be looking for their most sincere answers. But so often what churches essentially tell people about their norms and conventions is, "Take 'em or leave 'em." And unfortunately for the church, vast numbers of people keep choosing to leave 'em.

Finally, this book is about God. For so many people who are involved with or curious about the Christian faith, a discussion about God is badly needed, but it cannot be crammed down into a box or a creed or a book. It must be allowed to expand beyond traditional assumptions. Christians often say that humanity should obey God's law in the Bible, but we should never forget that it's humans who find it there. Humans interpret what the Bible says to them and therefore determine what God's law is for them. And no matter who you are, even after you read your Bible cover to cover, there will still be questions, confusion, and misunderstandings about God. That's because the Bible can't fully contain or express who God is. Our experience with God is marked by constant uncertainty. As the writer of the book of Ecclesiastes said, "Just as you cannot understand the path of the wind or the mystery of a tiny baby growing in its mother's womb, so you cannot understand the activity of God, who does all things" (Ecclesiastes 11:5). Humans cannot resolve or settle who exactly God is, what God does, and why God does it. But maybe we can learn to accept this uncertainty and focus on the expansiveness of our Creator and the good things that were placed in our hearts when we were created.

It can be difficult to talk about God today. Most Americans say they believe in God or a higher power, but a discomfort sometimes arises when people approach discussions of faith and spirituality. A palpable animosity even manifests in some instances. This is due, in large part, to the perceived arrogance of so many Christians who have spoken from positions of self-righteousness in the past. Tim Keller, a highly respected church leader and author, said that "each religion informs its followers that they have 'the truth,' and this naturally leads them to feel superior to those with differing beliefs."[2] Make no mistake, he is describing Christians. We cannot erase the self-righteousness and arrogance that is often displayed as people discuss religion, but we can work to move past it. Today we can promote inclusiveness, common ground, and connectedness as we engage in discussions about faith. Why wouldn't we? We've seen where sectarianism, side-taking, and self-righteousness have gotten us in the past!

As you enter the discussions in this book, my sincere hope is that you discover a more expansive faith. Religions often teach us to organize and resolve our faith down to the point where it fits into a neat and tidy box. But this makes it small, and it ultimately reveals shortcomings and faults in us. We can never organize and resolve God. If you believe in the Creator of the universe, then you must understand that God is not small. And as the apostle Paul said in a letter to people in the town of Ephesus, the kind of love that Christ preached and displayed is "too great to understand fully" (Ephesians 3:19). Please don't look for your faith to be neatly defined, resolved, and packaged. Instead, be aware of where it can lead you: to more expansive thinking, to a bigger heart, to incredible possibilities, and even to more questions.

Each chapter in this book contains questions, opinions, facts, and insights from some very thoughtful people. There is a lot to digest. You can read this book straight through or bounce around and return to different sections. Each chapter is like a module. It fits into the whole, but it can also stand alone. This is how I often engage my favorite books, articles, and podcasts. I might read or listen to certain sections several times over. This helps me digest their questions and insights. So read this book however you need to; just don't be afraid to dig deeply when you come across something that touches your heart, mind, or spirit. And if anything in this book catches your attention or sparks your curiosity, please read what other people have to say about it elsewhere. Dozens of authors, thinkers, and religious leaders are cited, and each of them can help you discover a more expansive faith. Please go read and hear more of what they have to say.

Finally, in everything you do, I urge you to think about life. Ask yourself what it means to really live, and how your faith in God might influence the manner in which you live. The Creator of our universe is unfathomably expansive—but also within reach *and* within us. In a world that is often shallow, hurtful, and unforgiving, there remains a higher power: a divine presence, a source of indescribable peace, strength, love, and healing. This is what the man at the center of the Christian religion showed us two thousand years ago. And he showed how beautiful, impactful, and profound our lives can be when they are rooted in these things. So let's start some discussions about how we can experience this kind of life.

PART I: DECONSTRUCTING

1. MY 21ST-CENTURY FAITH EXPERIENCE

I'd had enough. I was done. Done with church. I was done
listening to sanctimonious lectures on morality, bizarre descriptions of the afterlife, and naive assumptions about how some superhero deity will pull us from every bitter circumstance. I was done
hearing people talk about their spirituality in terms of kings, shepherds, and lambs. I was done watching people treat the Old Testament like a history book, like the stories were factual and important
simply because they happened. I was done being told that I needed
to believe something so my soul could be saved. Because what does
that even mean?

I was done listening to church leaders say that their interpretations of Scripture were set in stone, never to be refuted or reconsidered. I was done listening to people ask God to provide them with all
the comforts of a properly outfitted first-world citizenry. Most of all, I
was done being told that the Christian faith is mostly about a story
from two thousand years ago where God suddenly decided that I
deserved to be tortured, but then he figured that it would be sufficient
for his kid to get tortured instead, and that made everything wonderful. Because what does that have to do with my life today?

I have been around the Christian church since I was born, and I have been to church services all over the country. I grew up in three different Midwest states. I went to college out East and then served as a Navy officer, so I moved around a lot. After I left the Navy, I moved to New York City to become a professional musician, and I've moved three times since then. I've lived on the East Coast, Gulf Coast, West Coast as well as in the South, the Midwest, the Rocky Mountain West, and even Hawaii. I have lived in small towns, medium-sized cities, and the country's biggest city, New York City. And in every one of these places, I attended different types of church services. I also served as a music leader in many churches. I've been part of megachurches, community churches, and church plants. I've attended services in more Protestant denominations than I can remember, but also in some nondenominational and Catholic churches. As a kid, I grew up in Christian schools and churches. Like many of you, I have long heard the message of the Christian church at large in America.

My Christian faith has always been deeply important to me. It's part of who I am. It has given me hope, joy, peace, stability, connection, and healing throughout my life. But a few years ago I left the church. I just stopped going. The services I attended and the messages I kept hearing didn't really connect with my life. And while I disagreed with some particular beliefs in certain churches, it wasn't necessarily the beliefs that drove me away. It was what the experience lacked. And that was presence in my life. Sunday morning church services were nice; they were fine; but they hardly impacted the rest of my week. So I stopped going. And then something significant happened. Something happened that totally amazed me!

Not much changed. My life didn't change. My beliefs didn't really change. My desire to live well and connect with God sure didn't change. But one thing did change: my focus. I started to focus on how I wanted to live, who I wanted to be, and how I could become that person. I thought about how I interacted with people—in my family, my neighborhood, my workplace, and everywhere I went. And that's when I saw an opportunity for my faith to come alive. I learned that the Christian faith didn't need to be focused around a worship service. It didn't need to be centered around any formal activity inside a church building. Instead it needed to be centered around my life, all the places where I lived, worked, and interacted with people.

I was able to find all kinds of writings, books, programs, websites, and podcasts that sparked my curiosity about how the Christian faith could affect my life. I found authors and speakers and thinkers and practitioners who were already focused there. And I started having discussions with people over these topics. All kinds of people—not just Christians who attended church, but neighbors, friends, acquaintances, coworkers, people who had absolutely no interest in church, and even people from other religions! I had great discussions with people on these topics because how we live matters.

I found that the Bible wasn't just something that should be read out of obedience. And it wasn't important because it was historically true. It could be far more significant than that. It could actually have a place in my life. It could serve as a mirror for my circumstances, tendencies, and choices, and that made it a source of wisdom. Then I spent several months pouring over the Gospels—everything that Jesus said and did—and my perspective on the man at the center of the Christian religion changed. I found that he was keenly focused on helping people live more beautiful lives. He wanted to show them a better way. He wasn't just some abstract deity that needed to be worshipped. In fact, that wasn't his emphasis at all. Instead, he wanted people to pay attention to his message. And his message was overwhelmingly about how we can overcome our shortcomings, grow in maturity, care for each other better, uplift our communities, and do all of this with a connection to God. And that was awesome, because that's what I cared about.

Then I researched current trends and discovered that massive numbers of people have left the Christian church in the past several decades. Studies reveal that the percentage of our population that attends church regularly has steadily dropped this century.[1] Millions of people have left and are not returning despite so much hardship and uncertainty. In the midst of all the chaos of the twenty-first century, the church has actually become less influential. That seemed significant, as was the growing desire among our population to live well and practice a more effective spirituality. Studies revealed this growing trend, and I began to spot it everywhere. Increasing numbers of people are engaging in practices that foster mindfulness and spiritual connection. These activities matter because they help people live better. So then I wondered: Was this trend away from organized religion a negative phenomenon for humanity or was it actually an exciting new development?

Finally, I went back to school. I was in my forties, and I returned to college to get a master's degree at the University of Colorado. I spent two years taking classes with students who were much younger than I was, and I started having conversations with them. I quickly learned that these young adults are highly aware of how superficial our culture is and that they want to live in a manner that has far more meaning than their culture offers. They might be thinking and looking deeper into the experience of life than older generations ever did. That seemed significant. Young adults hunger for their hearts, minds, and spirits to rise out of shallowness and pettiness. They want to expand the experience of life. They want to have a good impact on the world. They want jobs where they can do this and lives where they can have this. And for many of them, their faith in God is real. Their interest in spirituality might even be increasing, but so few of them look to religious institutions for guidance. The number of people in the younger generation who choose to affiliate with a Christian church is alarmingly small compared to previous generations. Like me and millions of other people who have left the church, many young adults have concluded at some point that it just isn't worth their time or attention.

Facing these realities, I realized that I shared something profound in common with vast numbers of people: a value on both living well and connection to the divine. So I simply explored how my Christian faith could point my life toward good things. That's it. Good and beautiful things, like overcoming self-importance, living in the present, acting out of humility, growing in maturity, showing love to my friends and family, uplifting my community, and giving away my time, efforts, and resources in the interest of others. Jesus referred to these things as "good fruit" (Matthew 7:17) and Paul called them the "fruits of the Spirit" (Galatians 5:22-23). That's what I want my life to be about, and that's what I want my faith to be about. Not abstract concepts about my soul, sin, or events that happen after I die. That stuff can be interesting. It has some importance, but it has little to do with what happens at my work, in my home, or in my neighborhood. And for me, the Christian faith isn't worth pursuing if it doesn't matter in these places. I needed a faith that mattered in my life. I needed it to be relevant.

2. THE GREAT REJECTION

"You should start a worship service."

That's what he kept telling me. Did he not hear me?

I had just explained to this long-time pastor that I was planning an event for people who have no interest in a worship service. If they did, they would go to one occasionally. But they don't. I just wanted to plan an event that could serve them, where we addressed topics that are meaningful to them: resisting the incessant superficiality of our media culture, forming good relationships, being a positive influence, overcoming self-importance, making personal connections in a disconnected world, and dealing with anxiety, depression, and disappointment. You know, stuff that matters. This event would be on a college campus, for college students. It seemed like the kind of event that was badly needed among that age group. And if it was well-received, I wanted to add food and some hip music to the experience just to make it more fun for them. But I had no intention of making it a worship service.

"Well, I really think you should start a worship service," he said again. "That would be great."

"I don't think so," I finally said. "It's not a good idea because these people don't want to go to a worship service."

The Numbers

Research shows that more Americans leave organized religion every year. The Pew Research Center, Gallup, the Public Religion Research Institute, and the Barna Group have all published surveys that indicate a consistent, diminishing affiliation with the Christian church and a decrease in church attendance. This phenomenon is not new. It's been happening steadily for decades.[1] According to the Barna Group, at the turn of the century 45 percent of Americans were practicing Christians. Twenty years later, that number was down to 25 percent.[2] The Pew Research Center found that 78 percent of Americans described themselves as Christians in 2007, but that number dropped to 65 percent by 2018. Even when you consider population growth, the numbers in both of these studies equate to millions of people, and there is no data to suggest this downward trend will change.[3] To use a term from the Bible, *multitudes* of people have left the church. Some people do shuffle between sects within the overarching Christian religion, but every group is losing. Very few people left to join other religions, and almost none of them joined specialized cults.[4] Many factors can be attributed to the cause of this movement away from the Christian religion, but it remains clear that this trend is not likely to reverse.[5]

Church leaders and church members across the country have lamented this expansive departure for as long as it's been occurring. I have heard them express their disappointment and confusion across all the places I have lived. And I have heard many well-intentioned but ineffective solutions get offered up. Unfortunately, I have heard very few people articulate what I believe is the reason for this seemingly unstoppable departure. I believe it's simple. I believe it comes down to the message. The message preached by the Christian church at large holds little value to vast numbers of people. It just doesn't touch their lives. It's not relevant, and so it becomes unimportant.

Spirituality

On the other hand, it appears that spirituality is becoming more important. Studies show that more people every year consider themselves "spiritual, but not religious." This category keeps expanding. It's occurring across all generations but especially the younger ones.[6]

The word *spiritual* can imply different things. In their studies of spirituality in America, the Public Religion Research Institute defines spirituality as "being connected to something larger than oneself."[7] Brian McClaren, a well-known author and pastor, suggested that it involves "living in an interactive relationship with God and others as a daily way of life."[8] The Pew Research Center has completed multiple studies over the past two decades on spirituality, and they don't even bother defining it for people. They just ask if people "think of themselves as a spiritual person."[9] And most Christians would include an interaction with Jesus Christ, God, or the Holy Spirit in their definition.

Spirituality is many different things for different people. One thing we can take away from these statistics and from an observance of our culture is that interest in it is rising. Despite a vast and consistent departure from the Christian church, growing numbers of nonreligious people consider spirituality to be important today. So why are religious institutions failing to provide them with something worth engaging?

Think about that question: why are religious institutions failing to provide people with something worth engaging? It's a new kind of question. It doesn't allow us to place blame on the usual scapegoats: people who submit to sin, a depraved culture, or the devil. This question instead requires a bold and unapologetic look at religious institutions.

Here is what the question does not imply: that people are rejecting Jesus, falling deeply into sin, and becoming slaves to their evil culture. Some version of this sentiment is commonly heard within many churches, and it assumes that people who leave the church have entered some dark existence. Generally speaking, that's nonsense. It's not grounded in reality, and those of us who have left the church know it. It assumes that people who reject church services also abandon their beliefs and morals. It assumes they would rather live some kind of depraved life than one that is based in beauty and connection to the divine. Of course, this is not the case. If you ever talk to people who have left the church, you learn that it's over-whelmingly not the case. And statistics tell us that it's not the case.

This issue of people leaving the church might have very little to do with immorality, sin, or godlessness. Instead, the issue might have everything to do with what's being offered. If religious institutions don't offer something that is meaningful for people's lives, then people will reject those institutions. The church at large often blames people, culture, or the devil for the Great Rejection. But it's time we in the faith finally take an honest, critical, unfiltered look at what the church offers . . . and what it has failed to offer. It's time to openly and boldly acknowledge this Great Rejection.

More

The Pew Research Center says nine out of ten Americans believe in a higher power and that a majority of Americans identify with the God of the Bible. Three out of four Americans even talk to God regularly.[10] These statistics represent a far greater number of people than those who attend church. So for those of us who leave the church, the existence of God isn't always questioned, nor is our desire to interact with God. But the choice to identify with and participate in the Christian religion is certainly in question. The most pressing issue for Christian leaders is not how to prevent people from losing their beliefs and submitting to evil; it's figuring out why people lose interest in their version of religion. And perhaps it's not because people no longer care about God and living a life of faith, one that's full of meaning, purpose, and fulfillment. Perhaps it's because people *do* care, and that's *why* they leave.

Perhaps this is movement away from the Christian church is profound. Perhaps it's a grand statement, one that should not be underestimated. Perhaps it's even inspiring and uplifting for those of us who care about faith and living well. Perhaps it's not a statement that people want *less* meaning, purpose, and fulfillment in their lives; maybe it's a statement that people want *more* and that the church has failed to provide it.

Reggie McNeal's book *The Present Future* has served as a resource for many people, including church leaders, to better understand this movement away from the church. In it he reminds us that "values are demonstrated by behavior."[11] McNeal further points out that "a growing number of people are leaving the institutional church for a new reason. They are not leaving because they have lost faith. They are leaving the church to preserve their faith. They contend that the church no longer contributes to their spiritual development."[12] That is inspiring. That could explain so much confusion within church culture over this issue because it's counterintuitive to traditional reasoning: that people should subscribe to their version of faith. But McNeal's book was published over a decade and a half ago, and what has changed? It's still difficult for many Christians to accept that traditional, institutional beliefs and practices might actually hinder some people's connection with God.

The book *unChristian* by David Kinnaman and Gabe Lyons is another resource that has been used by church leaders to understand the Great Rejection. It contains extensive statistics and research-based conclusions. Unfortunately, some of its conclusions are evidence that Christians are easily blinded by loyalty to their traditional beliefs and practices. The authors create separation between people who leave the church and those who stay. They state that "millions of young outsiders are mentally and emotionally disengaging from Christianity."[13] They refer to people who depart the church as "outsiders." Before we even meet these people, they are separated from the more highly regarded "insiders." The authors further contend that these "outsiders" are "disengaging from Christianity," assuming that the Christian faith only exists in church organizations.

They go on to say, "A huge chunk of the generation has concluded they want nothing to do with us."[14] This statement is disappointing, and it's been expressed in churches across the country. Perhaps "insiders" should stop with the self-pity and take an honest look around. The issue is largely not about people disliking them; it's that their organizations might not offer anything meaningful or relevant enough to convince people to remain affiliated.

As counterintuitive as it seems, this Great Rejection is really about what the church offers. More specifically, it's about what the church fails to offer. It's ultimately about whether or not the message and the practices of the Christian church at large matters to people. And multitudes of people have made it clear that it does not. That's why I wanted to create an event for college students that addressed topics that are important to them. An event that opened up these discussions, provided encouragement, and created meaningful community for them could do a lot of good in their lives. It didn't need to be a worship service. They didn't want it to be a worship service. And so I didn't create a worship service. I just wanted to bring good things into their lives.

This Great Rejection happened over the course of decades. It continues today. From what I see in churches in my area and hear from people across the country, social distancing and the alterations that COVID-19 has forced on our lives will do anything but slow its continuation. They may even increase its rate. With this much bad news and this amount of consistent rejection, a reasonable person might think that the church would re-evaluate its message after so many God-fearing people have rejected it. Unfortunately, religious institutions often prove that they lack the awareness, the interest, and even the ability to redefine themselves. So we are left to witness the continuing trend of their diminishing significance.

3. THE GREAT DENIAL

Have you overheard or been part of this type of conversation at some point in your life?

PERSON 1. A lot of people have left the church. It appears they don't care about our message.
PERSON 2. Well, they should care.
PERSON 1. Yeah, but it seems like they don't. Why is that?
PERSON 2. I don't know. They should. Our message is important.
PERSON 1. Yeah, but they don't.
PERSON 2. Yeah, but they should.

I've heard this conversation in churches across the country. It's unfortunate that many people within the church are often not interested in answering the question of why people leave. Instead, they just hope that people will change their minds.

The Product

Consider this analogy. If a company manufactures a faulty product, a reasonable person would assume that the company will recognize and rectify that product's faults if it hopes for increased sales. That's pretty simple, right? The solution is to recognize and rectify the faults of the product. Everyone in the company knows that the product will remain faulty even after they invest in updates to the website, remodeling of office lobbies, streamlining of business practices, and the hiring of a new CEO who can really wow audiences at the annual investors' meeting. Improvement of these superficial qualities might excite a few investors initially, but consumers will continue to reject their product as long as it remains faulty.

Let's be very clear: the product of the church is its message. Church leaders preach a message that they believe will be significant for people. And people seek a significant message when they attend a church service. So the goal for both sides is the experience of a meaningful message. Churches might offer an attractive community of supporting people, but supportive community can be found anywhere. A church might also construct a new building with concert lighting and state-of-the-art sound systems. It might hire talented singers and an engaging pastor. It might produce high-quality, industry-level videos. But these elements are superficial. They are ancillary to the message, and ultimately they're just mediums to convey the message. And people keep leaving despite these improvements. So maybe it's time to admit that the product that a church offers, the product that makes it unique, which customers either buy or reject, is the message.

Newly refurbished facilities are wonderful. Charismatic speakers are great. High-quality music productions are awesome. Positive, supportive communities are fantastic, and they are so badly needed in our culture today. But they don't change the institutional message. Superficial and ancillary improvements may attract a number of people initially, but the trend of people leaving the church continues. That's because people will always reject a product that they don't care about. And in the twenty-first century people don't have time to waste on something that's insignificant in their lives. Especially in an age of growing interest in spirituality and meaningful living, the movement away from the church is so telling. People are actually looking for a product that will help them live better and connect with God, but for vast numbers of people, the church doesn't deliver.

This is an indictment of the stubbornness and unwillingness of churches to face their reality. One church leader recently told me that his denominational leadership advises its pastors to be encouraged if weekly attendance numbers just remain steady, as they have entirely given up on the prospect of growth. And the challenges that social distancing presents to church participation will not make this any easier to overcome. This is the reality of the Christian church at large in America.

Answers

Few churches have a working solution to the Great Rejection. And unfortunately, most of them discuss it exclusively with people who are inside their organizations. They have church meetings where worship leaders, elders, and members talk about the issue. They hire faith-affiliated business consultants to research the issue. They attend religious-affiliated conferences and workshops with other church leaders to discuss it. But rarely do they talk to people who left. They don't talk to the customers!

Isn't this astounding? So many churches look for answers, not where answers lie, but where they hope excuses can be found. Naturally their discussions result in validation of past behaviors and affirmation to continue their business with little or no alteration. It's especially curious that so many churches have taken on corporate business models within their organizational structures, yet they refuse to look at their product with a keen *business* eye! Consider what Reggie McNeal said on this topic:

An entire industry has been spawned to help churches do whatever it is they decide to do. Consultants, parachurch ministries, denominational headquarters, and publishing houses prod and push the church toward whatever the current fad is.

A spate of program fixes have consistently overpromised and underdelivered . . .

After decades of this kind of environment no wonder church leaders are a little skeptical about the "next thing" and why many feel that just about the time they catch up they fall further behind. But the mailings keep coming, the seminars keep filling up, and the conference notebooks keep stacking up on the shelves.

All this activity anesthetizes the pain of loss. It offers a way to stay busy and preoccupied with methodological pursuits while not facing the hard truth: none of this seems to make much of a difference. [1]

McNeal's commentary is harsh, but you can probably relate if you have ever served in a church. The absence of these multitudes from church services is a clear message that they don't care about the message that these institutions preach. Unfortunately, the response of church leaders is often, "Well, they should care." But alas, they don't. This is the Great Denial.

The Denials

There are two parts to this Great Denial. First, the Christian church at large has denied that their perceived foundational message might need an evaluation. Over the past several decades, millions of people have stopped attending church services. [2] Millions of people stopped buying the product that churches advertise and sell. And the overwhelming response from churches is the addition of more upbeat music, enhanced video presentations, charismatic speakers, and a more hip online presence. These are all wonderful developments, but they are cosmetic.

Many churches struggle to consider even the slightest changes to their product. Dr. Martin Luther King, Jr. criticized the Christian church at large for denying truths that it faced during the civil rights movement. He said, "Religion has sometimes rejected new truth with a dogmatic passion. Through edicts and bulls, inquisitions and excommunications, the church has attempted to prorogue truth and place an impenetrable stone wall in the path of the truth-seeker. The historical-philological criticism of the Bible is considered . . . as blasphemous, and the reason is often looked upon as the exercise of a corrupt faculty."[3]

The circumstances surrounding Dr. King's confrontation with the church were different than what we face today. The challenge in his time was to face a stubborn acceptance of racial inequality and social injustice. His reasons for critiquing the church were different, but he made a point that should be faced today. Religious institutions often zealously oppose any alteration to how they think and what they do.

The second part of the Great Denial has to do with the manner in which so many churches write off the people who left. People who leave largely end up being forgotten, and so they have diminished value. Millions of people have diminished value. They don't attend worship, they don't participate in activities, they don't donate, and so they are referred to as outsiders. Despite having the same spiritual curiosities as the rest of us, the same challenges and worries, and the same need for spiritual connection and community, they are considered outsiders.

Perhaps churches could at least ask this question to people who depart their congregations: What do you say? That's what Jesus asked in John 8:5. In fact, he asked this type of question throughout his ministry. He was constantly asking people to provide their most sincere opinions on all kinds of topics. Could it be in the realm of possibility that church leaders follow his example and ask outsiders what they think about beliefs, practices, and services? Could churches occasionally even cater to their beliefs instead of expecting conformity? Is that preposterous, or could it be a possible path for many churches to grow and even thrive in the twenty-first century?

It's a strange thing to consider for Christians who have spent their lives believing that their way of doing things is *right*. And it's hard to accept someone whose theological beliefs are *wrong*. But consider this very obvious statement: If you want to be irrelevant in the marketplace, ignore the needs of the customer. Was there ever a more simple and true statement for people in Western culture? And has there ever been a more critical time for institutional Christianity to think long and hard about it?

To be fair, many church leaders do check in with people who haven't shown their face on Sunday mornings in a while. Many church leaders keep their doors open in humility, hoping and praying that the departed will return. But these hopes and prayers are overwhelmingly that the departed will return to embrace the same product that was offered when these people decided to leave. So what has changed? This kind of naive hope begs the question, Why would the millions of people who decided to reject the product of the church ever return to buy it again? Maybe we already know the answer: they don't.

It's unfortunate that so many Christian leaders feel such pressure to remain within a singular, unwavering system of beliefs and practices. Historically, when a group of Christians gathered to form a community, quite often they felt a need to define and publish their theological beliefs. This is why so many different sects and denominations exist today. Christians have taken such pride in establishing their doctrinal boundaries—where exactly they sit in the great grid of theological beliefs and scriptural interpretations—that they end up promoting their differences, or to put it another way, exclusivity. And this is often how religious institutions are established, out of exclusivity. They are built on singular forms of beliefs and practices. They accept people who claim to accept their singular form, and then they make them members of the institution, or "faith clubs," as author and Catholic priest Father Richard Rohr once said. Like many people, I have actually been asked to sign papers and make public proclamations stating that I was in agreement with the exclusive system of belief of a particular church institution.

Reggie McNeal said, many "[church] leaders can't think of Christianity outside of institutional terms."[4] But can't we recognize that institutional thinking might not be the best approach to spiritual work? How can we fault anyone for leaving the church? Instead of wondering what's wrong with people who leave the church, maybe we should acknowledge their bold decision and even applaud them. They've actually made a decision to save themselves from man-made institutionalism.

Opportunity

This discussion poses big challenges for people in the Christian faith. But make no mistake, this is not about denying God, Scripture, or anything that Jesus said about how we are to approach this gift of life. This is about understanding reality and seeing where the Christian church stands today. Criticism can be painful, but it can also be a refreshing catalyst for the discovery of truth. Pastor Tim Keller wisely reminded us that "Jesus conducts a major critique of religion. His famous Sermon on the Mount does not criticize irreligious people, but rather religious ones."[5] Should those of us in the Christian faith consider following Jesus' example in this instance?

The migration away from the church in America happened over the course of decades. It happened across all states, all sections of the country. It also happened in Canada and Europe.[6] And it's still happening today. Churches often blame our shallow and self-interested culture for it, but that fails to explain the rising movement among the nonreligious toward spirituality and meaningful living.

There are many reasons why people leave the church, too many to list here. But one thing is clear, most people just found better things to do with their time. It might be that simple. Vast numbers of people just moved on to something else, and isn't it time that those of us in the Christian faith start admitting why? Isn't it time we start asking some tough questions about our message and why it doesn't seem to matter to vast numbers of people? And isn't it time we start thinking about the incredible opportunities that might lie ahead of us if we were to evaluate and even reconsider our message?

4. VOID AND OPPORTUNITY

S hortly before I finished writing this book, I shared its premise with a coworker. She and I had talked several times about faith. She had an awful experience growing up in a particular Christian denomination, and she wants no part of it today. So I asked her if she would read a short paragraph that summed up my book. It took her about thirty seconds to read it, and when she was finished, she said out loud, "I want to go to *this* church!" But I never mentioned anything about starting a new church. I don't even like the word *church* because it contains so much baggage today. Still I understood her excitement. Like me, she saw great attractiveness in a community of people that is not afraid to face our 21st-century realities, that values new discussions about how our Christian faith can matter today, and that centers our faith on how we live. My coworker got excited because she hadn't yet found that kind of community.

The Void

Interest in spirituality is growing. Huge numbers of people associate with the Christian faith, even if they don't attend church services. Our population's interest in living well is so immense that it spawned a booming, multi-billion-dollar industry of self-improvement products and programs. People long for content that can fill their hearts, minds, and spirits. Yet our culture seems to lack it.

Our culture seems to be devoid of content that intends to uplift us and help us grow into something better. American culture is largely a consumerist experience. We're encouraged at every turn to serve ourselves, please ourselves, and acquire more for ourselves. Consider also the effects that commercialism has on us. Commercial industries are built on profit, not our personal growth or well-being. They have to be, or they won't endure. And these industries are supported by advertisers, marketers, and brand publicists who are constantly barking at us. We are inundated and manipulated by ads that constantly pull us away from our thoughts as they shape sound, imagery, and language in the hope of stealing our attention. They simply want to distract us. Our minds can't focus on any meaningful or lasting thought when we're constantly told what to buy, what to follow, and what to think.

You may not feel like the self-centered, shallow, and small-minded thinking that our culture promotes directly affects you, but look no further than studies, statistics, and trends to see what a disservice it does to our already-suffering population. Look at the bickering and frustration displayed across social media. Look at the discontent and arguing across our politics. Look at the mental health problems we have despite all our electronic connections. Loneliness, anxiety, and depression affect alarming numbers of people. The size and scope of our mental and emotional challenges are astounding, and they are occurring across all generations, but especially the younger ones.

In our consumer and commercial culture there is a void of content that can truly help us live better. So a new discussion is needed, but these discussions rarely occur. Or at least they don't occur enough. And now an extraordinary opportunity stands before us to meet people's needs. Putting it in the language of capitalism, there is a need in the marketplace right now for communities that can have these discussions, but this need is not being met. Capitalists excitedly refer to this moment as an opportunity.

Where We Stand

So how do we approach these new discussions? I believe that the first thing we should do is recognize where we stand. Our world today is affected in many ways by postmodern thinking. Postmodernism is described in the *Merriam-Webster Dictionary Online* as "a radical reappraisal of modern assumptions about culture, identity, history, or language."[1] The Public Broadcasting System adds that it is "highly skeptical of explanations which claim to be valid for all groups, cultures, traditions, or races, and instead focuses on the relative truths of each person."[2] And the Modern Museum of Art in New York City says that it possesses a "refusal to recognize the authority of any single style or definition of what art should be; and the collapsing of the distinction between high culture and mass or popular culture."[3]

Postmodern thinking highly values individuality, but it also demands a questioning of any recent progress that has occurred. And today we see both the beauty and the futility of progress. We have seen philosophic, scientific, political, and financial systems rise and fall. We have seen organizations and individuals climb to success while subscribing to particular systems of thought, and we have seen them descend into irrelevance when those systems unravel. We see this process play out time and again in our culture, politics, and economic markets.

Today there is no shortage of moral, philosophical, and spiritual systems available as the answer for our lives. And one of the great virtues of our postmodern world is that we are not afraid to question traditional systems of belief. Nor should we hesitate to question traditional manifestations of our faith, such as our forms of worship and the way we form faith communities.

New challenges and opportunities arise in every new era. Reggie McNeal said, "The postmodern world will demand a new church expression, just as did the rise of the modern world."[4] The questioning of previously heralded frameworks is common to every era. So naturally it's part of who we are today. And fortunately, although perhaps not entirely coincidentally, we arrived here with nearly unlimited access to information. So we have no reason or excuse to blindly accept the assumptions of yesterday. Nor can we claim ignorance or naïveté. We can no longer hide. So much is in view now. And that means we can no longer avoid one grand activity: choice.

Choice

We have the God-given ability to make profound choices for our lives today. This is a freedom that God gives us. No longer do we have to attend the church that was planted in our neighborhood. No longer must we assume loyalty to the version of religion that we were born into. No longer do we need to stand reverently before religious institutions. We may ultimately choose to do some of these things, but no longer *must* we do any of them. Pope Francis made this very point. He said, "What does having inner freedom mean? . . . freeing yourself from your culture and its mindset."[5] Those of us in the Christian faith should understand that our *culture* includes both the secular and the sacred. It is our commercial culture as well as our communities of faith. We must be able to free ourselves from the mindsets of both if we are to live in freedom.

This expansive ability to make choices is our freedom to exercise, but it's also a huge responsibility. Our choices can change everything, but it takes effort to look across our choices and decipher which ones are best for us. Dr. Martin Luther King, Jr. challenged all of us when he said, "Rarely do we find men who engage in hard, solid thinking. There is an almost universal request for easy answers and half-baked solutions. Nothing pains some people more than having to think."[6]

In some area of our lives we have all taken the easy road, the path of least resistance, and we have learned to some degree that good results do not stem from inactivity. Rather, they result from effort and persistence. Today and always, every one of us possesses the great freedom of *choice*. Our choices affect how we care for each other and our communities. They can set us on wonderful, new paths of growth and discovery. Or they could point us back to traditional beliefs and practices. But the worst thing we can do is shrink from our freedom of choice. In a sense, that's how we ended up here, with all these questions about faith, religion, and the role they play in our lives.

Not everyone in the Christian faith wants to head in a new direction. Some people prefer to remain where they are, in the customs and traditions they have always known. Some people will also look to the past for guidance. I've been told by several church leaders that ancient practices are gaining popularity. These are practices and rituals that date back to the early medieval church and the small gatherings described in the book of Acts. But what the Christian church cannot do, if it legitimately desires an increasingly positive influence and presence in the world, is ignore the massive numbers of people who are not heading in *their* direction.

Light over Darkness

For some people, the thought of heading in a new direction is frightening. Some people believe that this newfound freedom will only lead to darkness, that if people question their beliefs and then choose not to follow traditional forms of worship, they will be separated from dependable moral foundations, good ethical behavior, and God. These people are the ones living in darkness because they choose to hold their focus there.

We all know darkness. We've all seen it and felt its debilitating force. We've all lived through trials such as economic recession, social unrest, social distancing, relationship problems, health concerns, and natural disasters. Some of us battle with mental and emotional challenges. Some of us have lived through violence and wars. And all of us have felt the pain of loss, the sting of death. Every human eventually learns that this gift of life is not dispensed without a guarantee of death.

Darkness is ever present. We will never fully escape it, but it need not discourage us because the battle of light and dark always has a predictable outcome. Light always reveals itself in darkness. Dr. Martin Luther King, Jr. said, "Darkness cannot drive out darkness; only light can do that."[7] John, the Gospel writer, reminds us at the very beginning of his book that "the light shines in the darkness, and the darkness can never extinguish it" (John 1:5). And the man at the center of the Christian religion said that if we just follow him—his way—then we will "have the light that leads to life" (John 8:12). So let us choose not to dwell on darkness. Instead, let us focus on so many areas of our lives that are starving for light and allow the light to reach them.

Shifts

As we look around our communities today, across every neighborhood, culture, religious background, social status, in every state and every political movement we can see people who want to live better. And this desire must be actively pursued because, despite all our digital connections, our culture has become terribly disconnected. But Americans are waking up to the reality of our disconnectedness and are beginning to engage more practices to overcome it. Fewer people may attend church services, but yoga and meditation have continued to rise in popularity among all ages.[8] Psychological therapy and mental health counseling have become a common practice for many Americans, especially in the younger generations.[9] Mindfulness is practiced in schools with convincing success in improving anxiety and performance levels for kids.[10] We can even fill our phones and tablets with apps that help us with these activities.

This is a wildly exciting time in our culture. A shift is happening where young adults are beginning to understand the value of connectedness. Jim Henderson, a longtime pastor and widely interviewed social-spiritual leader quoted by David Kinnaman in his book *You Lost Me: Why Young Christians Are Leaving Church*, described young adults today as "the great agreement generation." He found that they prefer to focus on areas of common understanding rather than areas of dissenting opinions.[11] This is not because they are weak-minded and lacking in solid opinions. Anyone who talks to young adults today knows that this is not the case. Younger generations value engagement and shared experience perhaps because they have been missing it more than previous generations. They value connection perhaps because their world fails to offer it. The craziest thing is that young people today could be more passionate than older generations ever were about exploring the power of spiritual connection in their lives, despite their absence from established religious organizations.

Your Opportunity

As you take advantage of this extraordinary opportunity, move with all the freedom, mindfulness, and authenticity that you can muster. Break out of traditional thinking. Think with all the openness, wisdom, and good intention that someone in the twenty-first century should think with. Embrace your God-given judgment about what you know deep down to be *good*. Allow it to bubble to the surface of your psyche and guide you. Allow your deepest awareness of the Creator of the universe to inform you. Allow your yearning for a connection with God to lead you through these fantastic, uncertain, open-ended times.

And if any part of you feels that you might be betraying something as you move forward, ask yourself what exactly that could be. Are you betraying your heart, mind, and spirit? Are you betraying God? Or are you betraying a man-made construct? Are you betraying the expectations of people and institutions? And if you are, then ask yourself whether or not that is okay. For some people, the choice to leave a religious community might not be an acceptable move right now. We have all kinds of reasons for remaining in communities that support, encourage, and protect us. But as you consider what God has placed on your heart, mind, and spirit, move with courage and sincerity. And if you do end up betraying the expectations of a religious tradition, then take heart: you have very much in common with the man who was at the center of it all two thousand years ago. This man,

Jesus, led a revolution against a small-minded religious culture! Seems like a solid idea to emulate him.

Pope Francis even encouraged us: "Think big! Open your heart!" he said.[12] "Have the courage to be truly happy! Say no to an ephemeral, superficial, throwaway culture, a culture that assumes that you are incapable of taking on responsibility and facing the great challenges of life!"[13] It can be assumed that Pope Francis was addressing our secular culture in this statement, but for many of us, religious culture also fails to equip us to exercise the responsibility of choice. Often times religious culture simply wants us to conform. The Pope, the head of the largest Christian institution, would not want us to make his institution obsolete in the future, but his words give us freedom to do just that!

Deconstruction

If we are to move beyond institutional thinking and the smallness of our culture in the hopes of discovering something more expansive, we may need to enter the process of deconstruction. Deconstruction, the systematic finding of faults in a set of beliefs, is quite easy to accomplish. Do not underestimate how quickly and effortlessly this happens. Know also that it also can be a very dark and unsettling experience. Our beliefs are based on upbringing, subconscious and conscious experience, paradigm, perspective, and choice. They are not entirely grounded in logic, scientific certainty, and concrete facts. They are filled with holes, soft proofs, guesses, and emotions. Our minds are powerful logical entities. They have no problem undressing our faith and exposing it against concrete, logical frameworks. Anyone can deconstruct their faith in a single sitting. And at some point this deconstruction process can leave people feeling lost, discouraged, empty, and alone. It can feel quite miserable.

If you ever find yourself wandering in the dark depths of deconstruction, I encourage you to remember that you are God's unique and incredible creation. No one in any part of the world or in all of the world's history is like you. And God created you with an expansiveness that runs much deeper than intellectual postulation. In the times where I questioned and challenged my deepest beliefs, I often had to stop and listen to my breath. I had to contemplate the miracle of my life, the blessings in my life, and the profound peace that I experience when I am connected with the divine.

This life is not solely an intellectual pursuit. When we let our heads lead, we often end up in a lonely place, for the mind needs no companions. But our hearts and spirits do. So thrust your heart and spirit into every step of this extraordinary opportunity. Know that you are a unique and incredible creation. And remember that the divine is in and around you.

5. TIME AND UNDERSTANDING

It was perhaps no coincidence that while I lived in New York City, Westerns became my favorite film genre. I never watched them as a kid. They were too boring. Their slow-moving plots lost my interest. But as an adult, I became captivated by the old, crusty characters who lived hard, discomforted lives. More than that, I was fascinated with the context in which they resolved problems: immersed in solitude, out in nature, with mountain or prairie landscapes to stare across for hours. They set their eyes on slow-crackling fires at night, slept under the starlit sky, then woke to the rising sun and headed off over trails on horseback. I realized that no matter what their challenge—violent outlaw bandits, government and tribal confrontations, financial hardship, or love interests—they had massive amounts of time to contemplate their problems. They had hours each day to mull over their options. They had loads of time to think about every aspect and possible outcome of the challenges that lay before them.

This was completely different from my life in New York. My wife worked regular hours during the day, and I was working as a musician, mostly at night. So during the week I spent my days taking care of our two little girls. I was changing diapers, feeding them, burping them, taking them to playgrounds, playdates, doctor's appointments, doing laundry, and all the normal stuff that parents do. When my wife would get home from work, we usually had a few minutes to visit, but then I had to head out and start my workday. It was awesome to perform music for a living, but it was chaotic and exhausting at times.

I played in a lot of Broadway shows in the evening. After each show I'd hop on the subway, completely charged up after playing for a theater full of people, and ride back down to Brooklyn. Then I'd walk a half mile uphill to our building, lumber up two big flights of stairs, step through the door of our lovely but little apartment around midnight, and the day would finally end. I'd relax on the couch, turn the TV on, and slow my heart rate down until exhaustion took hold and forced me to bed. Then around six a.m., and often earlier, the kids would wake up and we'd start another day.

During these years, I was constantly moving and my attention had to be pointed at the immediate priorities in front of me: care for the kids, meals, groceries, subway routes, guitar charts, conductor notes, and the hordes of people you clash with every day in New York City. If an important decision or challenge came up, it had to be processed quickly. I rarely had time for contemplation. My life moved so fast. Decisions were made amid the honking of cars, the pushing of strollers through crowded sidewalks, the roaring of subway trains, last-minute preparation for gigs, and the welcome applause of audiences. So living amid the hustle and cramped quarters of New York City, I longed for uninterrupted contemplation. I yearned for it—to hear what my heart, mind, and spirit were telling me. I attended church and prayed to God regularly but rarely took time to listen for any response. At times I felt like I couldn't even hear my own heartbeat over the noise of the city. In the midst of my busy life, I longed for what those old, crusty Western characters had: *time* to contemplate, meditate, and reflect.

Selah

Sometimes, when considering matters of deep importance, we need a brief respite from questions, discussions, surveys, and statistics. These topics, whether addressed internally or externally through conversations with others, can get heavy and confused. They can become complicated and heated, and sometimes we need to quiet our heads and allow our minds to settle.

There's a word in the ancient Hebrew language that can help us find peace in moments of confusion and complication. It's found in the original texts of Psalms and Habakkuk. The word is *selah*. It often occurs at the end of a section of great wonder, praise, or release of emotion. There is debate over its precise definition. Merriam-Webster defines it as "a term of uncertain meaning found in the Hebrew text of the Psalms and Habakkuk."[1] Some people believe that *selah* indicated a musical pause or a momentary relaxation of the production of sound. Some people relate it to the word *amen,* used to close out a thought and acknowledge its truth and importance. And some translations of the Bible omit this word *selah* entirely. But one of the most common and perhaps the most profound meaning of the word *selah* is simply "to pause."

The concept of pausing, or taking a moment, can be so helpful for us today. We benefit when we take a break from the complicated demands and chaotic schedules that define our lives. We benefit when we stop trying to fight and control emotional distress and simply allow it to run its course. We also benefit when we take time to digest whatever questions are swirling around in our hearts, minds, and spirits. This is how we often find peace with them. We can't force every issue to be resolved rapidly. The settling of deep emotional and spiritual issues often requires patience and longevity. Difficult questions often need time to unfold. And we honor the truths of complicated issues when we allow our hearts, minds, and spirits to spend time with them. The act of *selah* can be an extremely helpful tool as we look at our faith, in the hopes of building it into something more beautiful and present in our lives.

The Contemplative Mind

One way to pause and give our hearts, minds, and spirits time to process our most important thoughts is through contemplation. Father Richard Rohr speaks often about contemplation and refers to the practice of it as developing a "contemplative mind." He is keenly aware of how important it is in Christian communities and how its popularity is spreading.

> I'm encouraged by the rediscovery of the broad and deep contemplative mind, which for the first two thousand years of Christianity had largely been limited to monks, women, and mystics. It is not our metaphysics ("what is real") that is changing so much as our epistemology—how we think we know what is real. For that, we can thank a combination of insights from psychology, therapy, spiritual direction, history, and Eastern religions, along with the rediscovery of the Western and Christian contemplative tradition . . . . How do we find the path forward? Howard Thurman (1900–1981), a mystic who sought to make peace between religions and founded the first major interracial, interfaith church in the United States, urged people to "listen for the sound of the genuine."[2]

Of course . . . the sound of the genuine. This is what a contemplative mind can discover. It doesn't make hasty conclusions. Nor does it timidly grant moralistic authority to institutional narratives. The contemplative mind forms questions and allows them to be answered gradually. It engages both our understanding of scriptural verses and our knowledge gained from our lives, and it tumbles them through the tanks of our reason as well as our faith. What comes out might be divinely inspired, or it might not. We can't escape the limitations of our humanity, but beauty and fulfillment can be achieved in the *process* of contemplation. This kind of practice is a connection with God, because even when we question God, we are experiencing God's creation. We were created with these minds, these needs, and these questions. So of course we should "listen for the sound of the genuine." That just might be God in us.

Faith, with Our Involvement

Christians could learn a lot from the Jewish tradition of *midrash* as they learn to "listen for the sound of the genuine." Most Christians have never witnessed this tradition growing up, so it's not something they would tend to practice as adults. Christians tend to rely more on the deliverance of beliefs from outside sources than the forming of their own beliefs.

There are many forms of midrash. One common form emphasizes the practice of wrestling with holy text. Wrestling means the participant engages in prayer but also integrates their own knowledge, intellect, and life experience in the hopes of learning the significance of a holy text. This kind of practice cannot be done passively. The participant does not wait around for answers from heaven or expect that truth lies solely within the text. Rather, truth is revealed through the process of wrestling with a holy text along with the realities of life.

Overwhelmingly, Western Christian culture prefers not to wrestle with biblical text. We just want to be told what God says, in the simplest terms possible. In Christian culture we are often supposed to hear what the Word of God is *trying* to tell us, what our holy texts *intend* to reveal. It's what most of us experience in church services. It can also turn Bible reading into a passive experience, one that leaves many Christians feeling frustrated, unsatisfied, and sometimes guilt-ridden, because quite often we don't receive answers. Essentially the process fails, and therefore, we feel like we have failed.

It's ironic that when we wrestle with any important dilemma in our lives, we engage both our minds and our personal experiences. We do this with every decision, big or small: what car to buy, where to live, what job to apply for, which grocery store to shop at, what music to play at a party, etc. We might also pray over these decisions and seek God's wisdom and plan, but very few of us would completely shut off our brains and drop all our common sense when approaching them. The same should be true in our faith.

One concept that can help us wrestle with deep matters of faith is the Wesleyan Quadrilateral (WQ). The WQ was developed by John Wesley, the eighteenth-century leader of the Methodist movement in England. It points to something that should be obvious but is not always recognized in Christian traditions—that is, the role *we* play in the crafting of our faith. It highlights four distinct areas that work together in the generation of our spiritual convictions: Scripture, tradition, experience, and reason. The concept of the WQ can be compared to a table with four legs. It will not stand dependably if all four legs are not fully engaged.

This might be common sense to some people. But for many Christians who feel the burden of strictly taking direction from the Bible, it could free them from unrealistic pressures and expectations. Our traditions, our life experiences, and our own minds are always present in our readings and understandings of faith. This is true for every person who has ever read the Bible, including every European man in the Renaissance period and Middle Ages who crafted traditional Christian doctrine. But Christians are often told to ignore themselves, to ignore the world, and to ignore everything except that which is *in* the Bible. This sentiment can be heard in churches across the country. What we often forget is that it is *we* who find answers there. And each of us might find different answers.

The Latin phrase *sola scriptura*—Scripture as the sole or highest source for our faith—was touted by several great Christian thinkers, including Martin Luther, a sixteenth-century German reformer. It's nice to think that Scripture can provide an absolute, finalized answer on all of humanity's spiritual, moral, and theological questions, but it often doesn't play out that way. The more people actually read Scripture as their primary source document, the more they learn that they disagree on what it says, and the more they split corporate Christianity into different sects and denominations. That's what has happened throughout the history of the church. It happened because different people with different perspectives—reasoning, experiences, and traditions—made different conclusions on Scripture. Even within the Lutheran church, Martin Luther's grand legacy, there are multiple synods, and each of them has different things to say about how to interpret the Bible and how to carry out the Christian faith.

God gave us unique minds. God also gives us unique experiences, perspectives, and capabilities. Dr. Martin Luther King, Jr. once said, "God, who gave us minds for thinking and bodies for working, would defeat his own purpose if he permitted us to obtain through prayer what may come through work and intelligence."[3] And Jesus himself told us to "love the LORD your God with all your heart, all your soul, and all your mind." (Matthew 22:37)

Our minds must be involved in the forming of our own faith. If they aren't involved, our faith cannot be ours. And if it's not ours, then there may come a point when our faith is challenged and we find that it no longer works. How could it, if it doesn't belong to us? So at some point, we must look closely at our faith, and our religion, if we are to really know what we believe and why we believe it.

Wrestle

A lot of Christians have never considered questioning the foundations of their faith, and they refuse to question their religion. They want their religion to be set in stone. They want it to be resolved and right. This way they can depend on it without having to think about it. But of course we should use our God-given ability to think, question, and even criticize our religion. If we don't, how will we ever know that it's *right* for us?

The word *criticism* has two definitions. It can be an expression of disapproval, or it can be something much grander—a means of engaging and analyzing something to understand its merits and faults. Criticism, in the analytical sense, can actually be a means of discovering something! It can be a means of learning its most intimate qualities, allowing its importance to be revealed. If you ever want your faith to be right for you, you must know that your foundations are strong. And sometimes the only way to do that is to go through the uncomfortable process of criticizing the foundations of your faith.

As you wrestle with matters of faith, whether they be deep, foundational topics or simple curiosities, know that every question might not be answered. Sometimes it takes years to find answers. In some cases, a lifetime. And each of us will go to the grave with unanswered questions. This is an awesome aspect of the Christian experience, because it reveals that the experience of faith involves mystery! Just as the ways of God are a mystery, so is our faith. We must learn to appreciate the reality of mystery if we are to experience our faith throughout our knowing and our unknowing.

Clearly, we don't have all the answers in the twenty-first century. Even with our technology, industry, and connectivity, we are still riddled with anxiety, loneliness, depression, hurt, and resentment. In fact, all of our advancements have failed miserably to help us find meaning, purpose, and fulfillment. This might be one reason why so many people from other parts of the world are both jealous and dismissive of Americans. They see that we have acquired heaps of products, goods, and assets. They want these things, but they also see that we possess very little that is meaningful. As Dr. Martin Luther King, Jr. said, "The means by which we live are marvelous indeed. And yet something is missing. . . . Our abundance has brought us neither peace of mind nor serenity of spirit."[4]

In 1 Corinthians 2:2 Paul said that we must resolve to "forget everything." This can be difficult for Westerners. It's terribly difficult for people who live in the wealthiest nation ever. Perhaps it's easier for a camel to squeeze through the eye of a needle (Mark 10:25) than it is for a wealthy, privileged culture to embrace unanswered questions. Americans want answers. So do American Christians. They want it all to be figured out. They want to know who is right. They want to be in control. But so often we're just not. We don't always know why accidents happen. We don't know why so many people get cancer. We can't understand why deadly flu viruses spread across populations. We can't escape the holes, uncertainties, and limitations of this human experience. Sometimes the only way to find peace with them is to accept them and grow with them. As author and Bible scholar Peter Enns said, "an unsettled faith is a maturing faith."[5] Know that you are on the journey of faith when you continually need to seek answers. So have peace knowing that God sees where you are today, in all your contemplation and wrestling, and that God will be with you tomorrow. And when it ever gets confusing, don't forget to pause. Selah, for your heart, mind, and spirit.

PART II: I AM

6. BIGGER

We took my oldest daughter and her friends to a planetarium at the University of Colorado for her eleventh birthday party. The Astronomy Department gave a great presentation on the universe, at least what we know of it, and I was practically in tears through several parts. It's a good thing that it was dark for most of the show because I'm not sure my daughter would have wanted her friends to see me all choked up over the Milky Way. One particular part, where the presenter introduced the concept of the radio bubble, just seemed to undo me.

The radio bubble is the ever-growing sphere of our signals that extends from Earth past our solar system and into the Milky Way. About a hundred years ago humans began sending radio signals into space in the hopes of communicating with other life forms. So today our radio bubble extends about a hundred light years out from Earth. One light year equates to approximately six trillion miles. So our radio bubble today is a hundred times that distance, a number I can't even start to comprehend. Listening to the presentation, I was in awe that the human voice, even in the form of radio chatter or blinking lights, can reach that far out into space. Then the presenter zoomed out to a portion of the Milky Way, our galaxy, and the bubble looked like a tiny little dot. Then he zoomed out to the entire Milky Way, and the dot practically disappeared. Then he zoomed out past our galaxy to the billions of other galaxies, and the bubble was imperceptible. And the billions of galaxies that were shown are just the ones that our telescopes have detected so far.

I was in tears because of how small I felt. It was the most humbling sensation. My mind, my heart, my life, my understanding of how things work and what's important—it's all minuscule compared to what we have learned in just a few decades of high-powered telescopic research. And it made me think of God. It reminded me that if I believe in a Creator of the universe, then I must accept that God is the most expansive and unfathomable entity in the universe.

Bigger Than a Word

In all your spiritual contemplation and discussion, remember that you are not pondering a measurable, definable, quantifiable, doctrinizable object. We are not talking about something that can be summed up in a paragraph, or a chapter, or a book. Don't allow your mind to go small here. Allow yourself to appreciate the expansiveness and limitless nature of God.

Remember also that this spiritual entity has no name. God is the title we ascribe to the Creator of our universe because that word works best in the English language, but it is not a given name. When we address our Creator as God, we are simply using a linguistic tool. The ancient Hebrew language used other words: Yahweh, Elohim, and others. English translators used the word *God* because it works both in a literal and figurative sense. It helps us both to address and describe our Creator. God is our god. This word is useful for us, but it is still just a word that we use to refer to something unfathomable.

The name "I AM" is also used to describe God throughout the Bible, and what a helpful concept that is for the human mind. It's both a noun and a verb. It denotes presence, expansiveness, and constancy. As theological scholar and author Ilia Delio said, "It's a name that points to an incomprehensible mystery . . . to something ungraspable."[1] Our God does not exist within parameters. Our God has no physical description. Our God has no physical needs like humans do. Our God only exists. Everywhere. In everything. And the moment we attempt to define God, we lose our perspective on God's vastness.

God also cannot be placed in any gender category. As Reverend Wil Gafney stated, the ancient Hebrew text uses both the masculine and feminine to describe God at the beginning of Genesis.[2] So when someone states that the biblical God is a she, that person is correct. And when someone states that this God is a he, that person is also correct. But neither person is entirely correct. God is something far more expansive than individual masculine or feminine qualities.

God is not a father or a son. These words are simple metaphors that help our small minds understand the relationships that people have with God, but they don't comprehensively define them. God has no age. God doesn't live in the clouds or at some palatial address in heaven. God is not European, Jewish, African, Chinese, or American. God does not have a beard. God does not wear white garments. And God does not sit on a throne. These images don't define God. They are personifications—useful but inadequate tools—that humans use in their attempt to understand God.

So in all your spiritual considerations, remember that we are talking about an unfathomable entity. God is nameless, formless, and ageless. God is everything-ness. I like to use the term *Creator of the universe* because it effectively sets my perspective. I feel small next to it. It eliminates a lot of baggage that I could bring to the relationship. I am humbled at the thought of this spiritual force abiding both before the existence of all things and far beyond my years on earth.

Father Richard Rohr once quoted Howard Thurman, an author, philosopher, theologian, and civil rights leader. Consider what Thurman had to say about who God is and what God means to us:

> "The human spirit has two fundamental demands that must be met
> relative to God. First, He must be vast, limitless, transcendent, all-

comprehensive, so that there is no thing that is outside the wide reaches of His apprehension. The stars in the universe, the great galaxies of spatial groupings moving in endless rhythmic patterns in the trackless skies, as well as the tiny blade of grass by the roadside, are all within His grasp. The second demand is that He be personal and intimate. A man must have a sense of being cared for, of not being alone and stranded in the universe. All of us want the assurance of not being deserted by life nor deserted in life. Faith teaches us that God is—that He is the fact of life from which all other things take their meaning and reality."[3]

It's interesting that Thurman described *our* needs when discussing God. He didn't bother with hasty, detailed, overly confident personifications of God. He didn't flaunt what he perceived to be unquestioned theology about who exactly God is and what exactly God wants. Thurman exhibited humility and great insight into the deepest foundations of *our* faith when he described how we need to experience God. This kind of focus can help us remain humble in all our spiritual considerations.

Bigger Than the Human Mind

Our brains are powerful memory and computation machines, but they are small next to the Creator of the universe. They are limited in their capacity to understand the most basic attributes of God. For example, we have incredible difficulty comprehending infinity. Mathematical frameworks present infinity as a concept and show it as a symbol, but we cannot fully wrap our heads around it because it never ends. It can never be measured. In the same way, we are not equipped to understand our Creator. The infinite is real, but we can never fully identify it. This is God.

Neither can our minds fully comprehend eternity—moving backward toward the beginning of time, before the earth existed, and then moving forward billions of years into the future when there may be no earth. It boggles the mind. We lack the capacity to grasp eternity. This is God.

Our culture loves proof. We gain confidence when proof supports our arguments, especially proof that is based in numbers. We often feel that proof provides us authority, but proof and numbers only serve the physical world. The experience of our faith can only be described with metaphor. The man at the center of the Christian religion knew this better than anyone. Jesus attempted to help ancient Jewish people understand their connection to God through relevant cultural metaphors. In Matthew 13 he said that the experience of our faith in God is *like* a farmer who uses high-quality seeds, that it is *like* one small seed that eventually grows tall, that it is *like* the discovery of an unexpected treasure, and it is *like* that moment when someone fishing suddenly pulls in a huge catch. Metaphors might be best tools we have, but they still don't sufficiently define these experiences. So we must be open to something much more expansive than definitions, conclusions, and proof when we approach matters of God. Our minds can neither pin them down nor grasp their extent.

Bigger Than Great Cultural Movements

The Enlightenment, which began over three hundred years ago, put Western thinkers on a path that celebrated the human mind and its incredible capacities. The Enlightenment often placed rational thought above spiritual contemplation, and the church was not exempt from this great intellectual movement. Centuries of thought have been affected by it. The brands of Christianity that most of us practice today are thoroughly marked by Enlightened thinking, which is one reason why we ended up with so many sects, divisions, and denominations that boast definitive interpretations of Scripture.

Jared Byas, who has served as a pastor and professor of philosophy, says this about the Enlightenment's effect on Christianity: "These groups of thinkers and philosophers from the Renaissance and into the Enlightenment . . . they got excited about this idea that we can come to absolute certain knowledge ... [and] have a grounding that is incontrovertible, and that we can build incontrovertible truths on top of that and get to some sort of certainty. People like the certainty, but what we're holding up is an illusion."[4] Christians, just like Western philosophers, are notorious for their attempts to put God in a box. Defined. With parameters. Christianity has practically made a religion out of labeling, defining, and explaining God. But the Creator of the universe continues to surpass our attempts at quantification and qualification. We are continually confounded when we formulate academic and doctrinal frameworks for the divine.

We might actually go our entire lives and never actually discover anything other than circumstantial evidence that God exists. There may never be proof, and for many of us, that's okay. We might not need it. The language of facts and evidence (i.e., "beyond a reasonable doubt") cannot communicate what God means to us. It can't account for our awe and wonder over the spiritual realm. It can't explain why we feel a deep desire to connect with God. Facts and evidence have no place here. And that is beautiful. That is comforting, to know that our world is not just the three physical dimensions in front of us; that there is something else going on; that there is something constant happening in and around us; something expansive but also intimate; something with which we can connect.

Not everyone believes in a Creator of the universe, and that's perfectly logical. It makes great sense to believe that there is no god doing anything anywhere. No human could ever present clear evidence to convince a court of law that God exists. And with all the terrible things that happen every day throughout the world, the thought of a loving, present god is laughable to some people. Yet nine out of ten Americans still believe that God or a higher power exists.[5] And for those of us who feel a deep compulsion to connect with this higher power, let us remember that we are talking about the unfathomable—the Creator of the universe.

Bigger Than Institutions

Like every human who ever read an ancient text, religious leaders make interpretations and then call them truths. But a problem arises for many people when religious institutions declare that they discover ultimate, unquestioned, finalized truth. One of the definitions of the word *institution* is "an established organization or corporation."[6] When something is established, it is recognized as significant, and it possesses influence. Unlike the average person who reads Scripture, religious institutions do so from a vantage point of authority. They often leave little room for debate, and they have little inclination to entertain dissenting opinions. Their posture is one of assured correctness. So it is difficult for many Christians to break out of institutional thinking when it comes to faith, spirituality, and God because they don't want to disagree. Religious institutions place a great deal of pressure on people to conform. They have the ability to wield authority, whether it be legal, corporate, or moral. And they often create a culture of compliance. In fact, that's often the goal.

Dr. Martin Luther King, Jr. sheds light on the problem of conformity within Christian institutions. He said, "No where is the tragic tendency to conform more evident than in the church, an institution which has often served to crystallize, conserve, and even bless the patterns of majority opinion."[7] This statement should wake us up to the very real and often unhealthy pressure that the church puts on people to conform to its culture, beliefs, and practices. Dr. King also criticized people who fail to break out of institutional thinking: "Any Christian who blindly accepts the opinions of the majority and in fear and timidity follows a path of expediency and social approval is a mental and spiritual slave."[8]

We should never be afraid to question and dissent from institutions that position themselves as authorities on morality and abstract spiritual concepts. These institutions are as flawed as the people who congregate in their pews. Many religious institutions are guided by people of great faith, but they are still people. We should never accept an institution's declaration that their beliefs, doctrines, and dogmas

cannot (a matter of interpretation) and should not (a matter of morality) be argued. If we blindly assume that the faith that was handed to
us will agree with our hearts, minds, and spirits as we move through
the various stages of life, we will have very little agency with it. We
might not even recognize it if we were ever to actually question it and
open it up for evaluation. We can never truly own it if we had no part
in forming it. And if we have no ownership or agency with our faith,
how can we expect it to work and matter in our lives?

The twenty-first century, a period of great individuality and individuality consciousness, is ripe for questioning, debating, and, if necessary, deconstructing and reconstructing our faith. And if we stay
sincere and focused on what is good, we can grow and mature in our
faith no matter what questions arise. We don't need an institution to
approach God. And of course God doesn't require an institution to
reach us because God is so much bigger than institutions.

Bigger Than a Book

When considering the Creator of the universe, Christians look to this
book we call the Bible. It's the primary written source for the Christian religion. The Bible is said to be God's Word, and it is our holy
book. But understand that it reached us through human hands. And
every time you pick it up to read it, understand that it's being handled
by another set of human hands—yours.

The phrase *God's Word* or the reverse presentation of it, the *Word
of God,* is mentioned dozens of times both in the Old and New Testa-
ments. Most often it refers to some kind of spiritual truth, a covenant
between God and humans, or to Jesus, who is also referred to as the
Christ.[9] But the biblical use of this phrase isn't necessarily a reference
to a book. It's certainly not a reference to the Christian Bible, which
wasn't invented until centuries after the books of the Bible were written. Ancient Hebrew texts are referenced throughout the Bible, but
these are references to texts that existed in the Hebrew religion
hundreds of years before the New Testament was written, and not all
of them are even contained in our Christian Bibles.

Groups of religious leaders, such as the ecumenical councils starting in the fourth century, gathered to discuss and decide which books would be included in the biblical anthology, or canon.[10] These discussions went on for hundreds of years by various councils across Europe and Africa. As the religion began to organize, different sects recognized the authority of different councils,[11] and this resulted in the selection of different books for each group's biblical canon. The Ethiopian Bible contains 84 books, the Eastern Orthodox Bible has 76, the Catholic Bible has 73, and most Protestants use Bibles with 66 books. And, of course, Christians in every one of these faith groups believe that they have the *correct* version.

The apostle Paul said that "all Scripture is inspired by God" (2 Timothy 3:16). Other common translations use the term *God-breathed*. This verse is a grand statement of God's involvement in these ancient writings. It also introduces the debate over what exactly Scripture is. Again, Paul was not referring to the Bibles that we read today because he never lived to see one. And remember that Paul was not actually writing *books* for the Bible. He was writing letters to familiar people about relevant moral, spiritual, and political topics.

The debate over what exactly is to be considered "Scripture" has endured for thousands of years. Different humans have approached these debates in faith and sincerity, but they also exercised their freedom of choice. Ultimately, humans decided what ancient writings passed as Scripture. These humans certainly believed they were following God's guidance in their choices, but they had disagreements. So which Bible should we read today? Well, that's our personal choice. Every aspect of this debate over Scripture and the origin of the Bible involves human effort and choice.

Once we do choose the Bible that we believe most closely represents God's Word, we face yet another issue of human involvement. That is the issue of translation. For those of us who prefer to read in English, many options are available, including the Kings James Version, the American Standard Version, the New Revised Standard Version, and dozens more. Each contains unique words and phrases to articulate what the translators believed was present in the original manuscripts. Some Bibles are even translations of translations. In every case, translations are made by humans with distinct experiences, assumptions, and perspectives.

Translators, we hope, did their work without bias or agenda. We hope they did it in good faith and judgement. We hope they successfully found appropriate representation of both the words in those texts as well as the conceptual intentions of the authors; and of course . . . what God *breathed* into authors as they wrote their texts. But these translators were certainly fallible. They faced choices when they encountered words that lack an exact translational fit. They made decisions when they came across phrases, punctuation, and organizational indicators that did not translate perfectly into their language. Their fingerprints are all over the pages of our Bibles. This doesn't mean, however, our Bibles can't be trusted. It doesn't mean we shouldn't read them, contemplate them, and use them as a tool to better understand the challenges of our faith. Our Bibles help us know God and they help us know ourselves. They can point us in beautiful, impactful, and profound directions. In fact, they can even become more significant in our lives when we actually understand how they reached us.

The study of the challenges and intricacies of translation is called *hermeneutics*. Some people feel uneasy with hermeneutics because they want their Bibles to serve as a perfect, unquestionable sources of God's wisdom and purpose for their lives. But hermeneutics can introduce endless and wonderful discussions for Christians. Our God might be characterized by perfection, but the same cannot be said for every sentence that we read in the various versions of our Bibles. Often times we assume the words on the pages of our Bibles have authority simply because they are there. And many times we assume that God wants us to receive these particular translations simply because we have them. But today we have access to different versions and translations of the Bible. More than any other time in history, we now understand that there are inconsistencies and translational limitations in our Bibles. We cannot escape the fact that our Bibles might

send us down distinct and sometimes misguided paths of interpretation.

The word *repent*, for example, is common in the King James
Version. It is derived from the Greek word *metanoia*. Certain Christians sects have made the practice of repentance a hallmark of their
tradition. Others have not. Perhaps that's because there is another
translation, or meaning, of *metanoia*, which is to "change one's
mind."[12] Changing one's mind is a far more involved process with far
greater ramifications than just saying we're sorry. The two concepts
can be related, but one is essentially an urging to be honest in the
accounting of our thoughts and behaviors, and the other is a choice
that can change every aspect of our emotional, physical, and spiritual
lives. Perhaps when we read that Jesus tells people to "repent" in
Matthew 4:17, some people miss out on a life-changing practice of
self-transformation in the interest of just admitting their mistakes.

Consider also one phrase in Matthew 28:19: "go and make disciples." English translators selected these words from an ancient Greek
text, but what does it mean for us today? How do we interpret it? By
"going," are we supposed to preach to crowds of people on the street?
Should we knock on every neighbor's door? Hold up signs at a football
game? Spray-paint overpasses? Are we all supposed to travel to distant
lands, like missionaries, and preach? And how do we "make" someone
a disciple? Do we speak convincingly to them? Do we offer a course in
discipleship certification? Or do we come down on them ruthlessly and
force a particular culture of Christian discipleship through violence
and brutality, like so many Christian leaders did in the past? And what
exactly is a "disciple"? Is it someone who studies Jesus, like a scholar? Is
it someone who sells all his possessions and walks from town to town
preaching? The questions never end over this four-word phrase. The
crazy thing is that we haven't even gotten into the six words that follow
it. The sentence goes on to say, "go and make disciples of all the nations,
baptizing them . . ." These next six words open up larger debates over
what "all the nations" means and what the practice of baptism entails.

Do not underestimate the influence this phrase has had on Christians over the centuries. It is often received as a command from Jesus, and so it is received, albeit in different ways, with the utmost seriousness. But every single person who ever lived might come away with different guidance for their life. So when someone says that this phrase *means* something, they imply that it means something *to them*. And of course it might mean something completely different to everyone else. Our interpretations, even when grounded in prayer and communication with God, are still *our* interpretations. The same is true for the interpretations of other people, all of whom might be grounded in prayer and communication with God. And our interpretations of the Bible might change as we move through life, the same way that our perspectives change. Your values and beliefs about the world as a twenty-year-old will change as you reach other ages; so might your Christian beliefs.

One interpretation of the Bible cannot always work perfectly as a rigid, singular system of comprehensive guidance for all of life. And this is actually a wonderful thing, because it means that our Bibles are far more profound than a simplistic answer book. Throughout our lives they can serve as a mirror and a tool to see and understand ourselves, our lives, and our interactions with the divine. But of course our lives do not exist in a book, nor do our experiences with the Creator of the universe. So we must make wise choices when we approach our Holy Bibles, and remember that God is so much bigger than a book. We should also understand that when we give authority over our lives to a book, then naturally we will set that book on a pedestal, like an idol. And we often end up worshipping the book instead of our unfathomable Creator.

Bigger Than Religion

Finally, as much as some people might hate to admit, we must never forget that God is bigger than our religion. Merriam-Webster defines *religion* as "the service and worship of God or the supernatural."[13] Religion combines our beliefs and practices as we attempt to understand and connect with God. Part of this book is a critique of the

Christian religion, but it does not write it off. Religion can have a beautiful influence on our lives. Engagement in corporate beliefs and practices can help us connect with God, but the same is true for people with different corporate beliefs and practices. God connects with people everywhere, in every part of the world, inside the structures of every religion. The Creator of the universe is accessible to all people everywhere. Not just Catholics in Boston, Lutherans in St. Louis, Southern Baptists in Nashville, or Mormons in Salt Lake City. All people. Everywhere.

Many people experience the Creator of the universe, but with a different name, through a different language, and in the context of different practices than ours. We might refute them. We might look at them like they're nuts. And they might refute us. They might look at us like we're nuts. Our God is bigger than all of this. The Creator of the universe is bigger than our comparisons. Our Creator is bigger than all the various religions scattered across the earth, including ours.

Perhaps we should take Jesus' words seriously when he said that "anyone who does God's will is my brother and sister and mother" (Mark 3:35). And perhaps he was speaking expansive truth when he said that "anyone who is not against us is for us" (Mark 9:40). As Father Richard Rohr pointed out, perhaps we have also not spent enough time contemplating Jesus' words when he said, "I have other sheep, too, that are not in this sheepfold" (John 10:16). What an incredible thought: that anyone can know and love God, even if they don't belong to our sheepfold, sect, denomination, or religion.[14] And as Paul said several times, God is not just the God of one particular community or religion. God is the God of all people, no matter what religion we are born into or end up practicing (Romans 3:29).

The concept of nonexclusivity is difficult for many Christians to accept, but our God is capable of connecting with anyone anywhere. And isn't that absolutely awesome? We can find such comfort in the notion that we possess a deep connection with all kinds of people who at first appear strange or foreign. This connection could eliminate so much fear, insecurity, hate, and so many small-minded reactions that we have to people who are unfamiliar to us. This can relieve a burden that we so often carry: the tendency to skittishly protect ourselves from people we don't understand. It could provide peace and confidence in the knowledge that we shall not be overwhelmed by petty differences in skin color, language, traditions, or even beliefs. It can remind us just how small we are in the vast universe that God created.

It's strange that Christianity fights this concept. It's telling about the level of insecurity and small-mindedness that the church possesses regarding who can experience the Creator of the universe. If the greatest commandment in Matthew 22 is to love God and other people—if that theme is so central to our faith and spirituality—then that is something around which we can build our lives. And anyone in any part of the world can build their life around that concept. In fact, people already do. They might use a different name for God. They might speak a different language. They might form different practices. But they are living out what Jesus recognized as the most important theme for our lives. And if it is the most important theme, then it trumps all others. It reduces all the debatable details about beliefs and practice to less significant semantics.

As much as we love our religion, it is small compared to God. God is so much bigger than our language, our minds, our cultural movements, our institutions, our Bibles, and our religion. And that's reassuring, because no religion is perfect. But our God is.

7. EVERYWHERE, EVERYTHING

M ost people I knew growing up went to church every single Sunday. We loved our churches. Most of our friends were there, so we would always visit afterward. We had refreshments and snacks, and we spent time with each other. But I noticed something as a kid that made me curious, and it continued into my adulthood. No one really talked about the sermon after the service. The sermon, message, or homily was supposed to be a central part of the church service. It was supposed to be where our faith grew and expanded. It was where preachers passed on valuable, life-giving messages. But no one really talked about it afterward. Instead, people talked about their work, school, kids, sports, vacations, and other happenings in their lives.

This always made me curious. Was the message not valuable? Did it not matter? Did it not contain relevant, life-giving content? Were we just not comfortable talking about profound concepts with each other? Or was it enough to experience it while it happened and then move on?

I was no different from anyone else. Even as an adult, when church services ended, spiritual talk pretty much stopped. Post-service conversations landed back in the middle of my daily life. But in recent years, as I realized how important it was to have my faith *in* my life. I realized that I had to approach this whole thing differently. The answer wasn't to force anyone into deep, spiritual conversations. But if the version of faith that my church was promoting didn't matter even five minutes after the service ended, something needed to change. I needed to change how I looked at faith, and what I was looking for in it.

Facts, Studies, and Statistics

The Pew Research Center has suggested that almost 90 percent of Americans believe in God or some sort of higher power, and roughly 75 percent of Americans associate with the Christian church.[1] But with our busy lives and tightly packed schedules the world of the divine might rarely cross our minds. Some people wake up every morning to a disciplined routine of prayer, reading, and meditation, but most of our routines are driven by jobs, family, housekeeping, and physical needs. We are bombarded throughout each day with messages from our culture encouraging us to remain in the physical realm. Buy this, watch that, read this, plan that, eat this, drink that. Then at night we often unwind with entertainment on a screen, in most cases further avoiding the divine realm. Few voices in our lives today encourage us to reach beyond the three physical dimensions around us. But even if we rarely engage these divine realms, they still exist. And they are accessible.

The Creator in Our World

For many of us, God is real. God is also present. Even if we haven't set foot in a church, prayed, or talked about our faith in years, we can still find ourselves in moments where we experience God's presence. Something happens, and it's outside the physical realm. It's beyond our understanding. These experiences take place throughout our lives. They might happen through nature or art. They might occur in the presence of someone we love. They might happen in a situation that miraculously worked out favorably for us or in the midst of an awful experience.

The Pew Research Center also revealed that 75 percent of American adults say they regularly talk to God or another higher power in the universe. As much as we hear that our culture is secular, most of the population still attempts to connect with God at least occasionally. And 30 percent of Americans even say that God talks back to them.[2] Not everyone hears God's *voice*, but these statistics say something profound about our nature. We have an innate desire, and perhaps a need, to connect with something greater than ourselves. And the vast majority of us engage it, regardless of our attendance at religious services.

Carl Jung, the famous Swiss psychologist, said that the idea of God is ingrained in us. Jung believed that the notion of God and our beliefs in spirits are an archetype that is "universally present in the preconscious makeup of the human psyche."[3] This is a complex subject, and this book offers no opinion on the origination of our beliefs in deities. Those discussions belong in a different kind of book, but Jung's theory is supported by statistics. The number of people who believe in God or a higher power in America reveals how common and important this concept is for humans.

In All Things

Those of us who believe in God and want to interact with God must learn to communicate with God. Communicating with God is a practice that can grow in richness and effectiveness over time, and there are so many places and activities where this can be nurtured. But of course it doesn't have to be in a church. For many of us, church is just one of many places where we experience our Creator. Many of us feel God's spirit move through music, dance, meditation, the spectacle of nature, and even in moments of pain.

Of course, we experience God when we feel joy, love, and comfort. But our Creator is in and around us in all circumstances, not just the pleasant ones. Our Creator can instill in us a miraculous peace during moments where we should be crushed by anxiety, anger, and pain. Many of us know this from experience. We have felt emotional or physical healing in times where such healing should not have logically occurred. And sometimes God does not deliver us from harm. Sometimes God allows suffering to remain with us. Sometimes we are simply not rescued, but we can still experience God.

When I served in the Navy, our nation got involved in two wars. I knew men and women who were killed in Iraq, Afghanistan, and over the bodies of water that surrounded those places. I know families with massive holes in their hearts because of combat casualties and aviation accidents. I've been in the houses of mothers, fathers, siblings, and fiancées who crumbled at the news that their loved ones were gone. They were crushed. Their lives turned empty and dark. And nothing eased that pain. God did not remove it or rescue them from it, but many of them still felt the peace of our loving God.

Just like millions of people, my life has also been affected by cancer. I have seen loved ones suffer as they struggled both with cancer's symptoms and with modern medicine's treatment of it. My oldest daughter was diagnosed with cancer on her first birthday. She underwent surgery and chemotherapy over the following weeks. She was an infant, completely innocent and vulnerable, yet a tiny and threatening tumor grew inside her kidney. The surgery and following treatment brought her so much pain. It crushed us, as her parents, to see that happen. Thank God she survived.

During that period of our lives my wife and I spent a lot of time up on the ninth floor of Memorial Sloan Kettering Cancer Center in New York City. That was the pediatric floor. Our daughter was treated there, and we met other beautiful families whose kids were being treated. We met families of all races, languages, and religions. But some of those kids didn't survive. And the pain those parents felt, and still feel today, has got to be unbearable. I have an inkling of it because of the many times I sat and considered the possible outcomes of my daughter's cancer diagnosis. Just the prospect of that feeling is the most awful thing I can imagine. Those parents who lost their children were not rescued from their pain. They never will be. I hope and pray they learn to live with it, but they were not spared from it.

Many Americans also live with neighborhood violence or with illness. Some people live with injuries to their bodies or their psyches. These experiences can often be managed or treated, but they might never leave us. Sickness, injury, emotional damage, failed relationships, unemployment, poverty, hunger, and the death of loved ones are common experiences for humans. We may not be rescued from them, despite our best efforts, wishes, and prayers. We can ask God to give us strength and peace as we cope with them, but God does not always deliver us from them. Still, even in the midst of our darkest hours and most painful episodes, God is near and can often be felt.

My disposition toward God during my daughter's cancer ordeal was rarely that of gratitude or joy. God was often the recipient of some very heated outbursts. At times I was resentful of the pain that this creation could deliver without remorse. I was so hurt, and I let God know every bit of it. God heard the ugly thoughts that swirled in my head. God also received some harsh words from me. I didn't hold back. And over time, as the pain subsided, I realized that I had experienced something profound. I had experienced the presence of God in those horrible circumstances. This presence was always near. I was connected to it, and I rested upon it, even in my bitterness and pain. But this connection would not have been possible had I not been authentic before God.

Soren Kierkegaard, a nineteenth-century Danish philosopher, expressed great wisdom regarding authenticity before our Creator. He spoke about it in the context of *sin*. He said, "Sin is the despairing refusal to find your deepest identity in your relationship and service to God. Sin is seeking to become oneself, to get an identity, apart from him."[4] What a helpful concept. Kierkegaard expanded the concept of sin to something much greater than just bad deeds. He related it to a lack of authenticity, wholeness, and presence. We are not ourselves, we are not whole, and we are lost when we are not sincere with God.

Whenever you experience pain, give it to God. And when I say *give it*, I don't mean what churches often preach: just hand over your pain to Jesus who will promptly make it disappear and replace it with perfect happiness. Humans can't always just pass off their pain. Pain is something that resides in us, and sometimes only the passing of time reduces it. When I say *give it* to God, I mean do not hold back. Unleash it on God, like when Jesus lamented despairingly in Matthew 27:46, "Why have you abandoned me?"

Communicate all your pain, anger, and resentment. If you must, yell at God and don't be shocked if disrespectful words come out of your mouth. Hold nothing back! Our God is not small. Our Creator will not shrink in the presence of human emotion. Whatever ugliness you reveal is minuscule in comparison to the unfathomable spiritual force of God. And when that moment of anger and ugliness passes, you can take comfort knowing that your relationship is grounded in sincerity. You may end up asking forgiveness for your harsh language, but at least you have revealed yourself. You have not hidden. You have stood before God with your fullness—the good, the bad, even the ugly. Intimate and trusting relationships cannot be built without authenticity. This God who created our beautiful and unforgiving world just might be familiar with every emotion that can ever well up inside us. So don't hide them. Experience them *with* God.

Every Moment of Every Day

We move in a fast-paced world. Each day our focus shifts from task to task. Stimulant to stimulant. We pride ourselves on productivity and the completion of tasks. High productivity often makes for a good day, so it can be difficult to squeeze moments into our life where we experience a connection to the divine. But what a tragedy it is to go through life assuming that it should be spent completing tasks in the physical realm. What a waste of our short time on Earth. Pope Francis made this point:

> The frantic pace of modern life seems to seal away all hope and joy from our daily lives. The pressures and the powerlessness we

experience in so many situations seem to shrivel our souls; the countless challenges we face stupefy us, paralyze us. The world is speeding up to build—in theory—a better society; yet paradoxically at the end of the day there is no time for anything or for anyone. We have no time to spend with our families or communities, no time for friendship, for consensus, or for reflection.[5]

This is an unfortunate reality for many of us, but take heart and remember that God is not absent. God has not departed. Know that even when your life is mostly comprised of busy work, God is still there. God has not left the scene. God has not retreated. God has not fled your home, your workplace, your car, or your doctor's office. God is in and around you. Every moment of every day. No matter what you do, no matter where you go, and no matter how fast you move, the Creator abides in everything.

Author Rob Bell made this point in his take on the story of Moses and the burning bush in Exodus 3. For many of us who grew up in church culture, the most profound part of this story was the bush that was burning without being consumed. This miracle might have been the high point of this story. But Bell helps us see a side that actually relates to our lives today. Here's what he said: "God tells Moses to take off his sandals, for the ground he is standing on is holy. Moses has been tending his sheep in this region for forty years. How many times has he passed by this spot? How many times has he stood in this exact place? And now God tells him the ground is holy?"[6]

Bell's questions are insightful. He points out that the unimpressive ground that Moses trampled possessed God's divine presence. That ground which was probably dry, rocky, and passed over many times without a thought for the divine—that ground was holy. But happy-go-lucky Moses never thought about it. How similar is that to so many moments of our lives? How many places have we stood in or passed by without a thought of the divine? How many rooms do we enter where God might present an opportunity to connect with something divine, but we don't notice it? And how often do we just go about our business assuming that the only thing worth tending to are the three physical dimensions in front of us? Meanwhile, so much else is happening.

God is everywhere. God is in everything. And so rarely do we comprehend it.

Works of Man

God may never come to us or speak to us in a convincing manner. We might feel God. We might sense God. But our lives are rarely, if ever, affected by miraculous visions or visits from spirits. So let us now consider this question: When does God give inspiration to humans in their work? Worded another way: Is the Bible the only divinely inspired writing?

Some Christians recognize the Bible as the only holy text on earth. This is because councils of religious leaders decided many centuries ago that certain books were *inspired* by God, and those books were included into their Bible. Other books, while important, were not included. But different councils came to different conclusions on what books were inspired. The book of Revelation, for example, didn't make the cut until the year 395, after several councils rejected it.[7]

The question of which ancient writings were inspired can easily become tangled in semantics. The same is true for writings and works of art that are produced today. Just like all those old councils questioned different texts, so should we do the same today. Books, letters, newspaper columns, blogs, brochures, lyrics, poetry, and fictional writings—don't we also experience God when we engage with many of these sources? Some people might be uncomfortable with this question because they feel that it compromises our reliance on the Bible, but the experience of our faith is so much bigger than any one book. This question should be present in our life because it has to do with all the different places where we experience God. And if the experience of God matters, then naturally we will value the many different activities and places that foster it.

All kinds of writings and productions move us today. Consider the people who are cited throughout this book: Brian McLaren, Wil Gafney, Pope Francis, Dr. Martin Luther King, Jr., Father Richard Rohr, Rob Bell, Dave Kinnaman, Deepak Chopra. These people are bold, committed thinkers about the spiritual world. Together they have published hundreds of writings on the subject of spirituality and faith. And they have guided many people on their spiritual journeys, as do other authors, pastors, composers, songwriters, and thinkers. We often feel God move through us when we engage their works. Our faith grows and our connection to God deepens, so the experience we have with them is often divine and holy. Might that mean that those works were divinely inspired? To some extent?

This question is for all people, and it can apply to all kinds of writings, publications, sermons, podcasts, art, music, film, business models, architecture, landscapes, and so many creations of man. And we can even turn that question toward ourselves. Does God inspire us in our work? Does our approach to a project at the office reflect the presence of God? Are our conversations ever inspired? Are our dreams or creative ambitions conjoined with God? How do we know if they are? And for the ones that are, exactly how inspired are they? In what ways are they inspired?

These are questions for your life. They matter because they define your experience with God. They can manifest your connection to the divine. So invite them into your life as you consume books, podcasts, articles, film, music, art, architecture, and anything else that mankind presents to you.

Nature

Romans 1:20 recognizes the exciting concept that God is revealed in nature. It says people can "clearly see his invisible qualities." Think for a moment about the doors to spirituality that these verses open up for us. Nature is God's creation—from earthquakes to DNA strands, space and astrophysics, psychological complexities, plants and animals, evolutionary developments, and weather patterns. From the expansiveness to the minuscule—this is the work of God, and we can experience and know God through all of it. And perhaps we've always known this. Perhaps we are more deeply connected to our Creator than we ever realized because our eyes have seen and experienced God throughout our lives.

The brochure for the Christian Reformed Church, a denomination related to Presbyterianism, states that "God has revealed himself through two books: the book of Scripture and the book of nature."[8] Of course! And if God is revealed in nature, then why wouldn't we look *to* nature for lessons for our hearts, minds, and spirits? Why wouldn't we look *to* science? Why wouldn't we look *to* our experiences? Not holding them up to be idolized, but as part of our expansive understanding of our Creator.

This biblical concept could lead us toward expansive new connections with our Creator. Does swimming in the ocean, or watching the sky at sunset, or spending a night camping up in the mountains serve as a real spiritual experience? Is the same true for rocking a baby to sleep? Does squeezing a handful of soil connect us with God? Does a thirty-minute walk with our spouse help us to connect with God's creation . . . and with our partner? Are these valuable spiritual experiences?

Of course, they could be. But are they? Do we allow them to be? How often do we invite a connection with our Creator through them?

So Much More

Do you see why religious organizations so often leave us lacking? Do you see why weekly sermons that solely focus on a Bible story are often not big enough for us? They're one good aspect of our faith, but they aren't big enough to teach us or show us all that we can know and experience. There is great value in Bible engagement, but our experience with God is so much bigger than words from a book. As helpful as they are, our faith can be so much bigger than scholarly conclusions about ancient stories. This very discussion does stem from Romans 1:20, a passage in the Bible, but we should remember that it leads us away from the singular practice of reading ancient texts. It leads us out into the world, into this incredible creation.

From the minuscule to the expansive, from mathematical models to music to medical mysteries, God can be found everywhere in our universe. And our unfathomable God can connect with us in all parts of our lives, if we desire it and open our eyes to it. If any Christian is still leery of looking beyond the Bible and into their life for a connection to God, remember that Bible writers·reminded us dozens of times that God's nature is written in our hearts (Jeremiah 31:33; Psalm 37:31; Romans 2:15; 2 Corinthians 3:3). It's in us. And Jesus never pushed anyone toward a strictly text-based faith.

Our God is everywhere. God is in everything, including us. And if we really believe this, then shouldn't we start knowing God everywhere? Isn't that what people of faith ultimately want—God in all parts of our lives? If not, then maybe you should ask yourself what your faith really means to you. But also know that you can never truly escape God. You could leave our solar system and God would still be there. You could leave our galaxy and traverse every galaxy that our telescopes can and cannot detect, and you would still be in the midst of the Creator of the universe. So look for God. Everywhere. In everything.

8. NOW

I went through Navy flight training when I was in my early twenties. The first helicopter I was trained on was the TH-57B, the Bell Sea Ranger. The first several flights in the Sea Ranger were mostly meant to help the student learn to operate the machine safely and smoothly. Unlike fixed-wing airplanes, helicopters can move in all six directions: up, down, left, right, forward, and backward. The nose and tail can also rotate right and left. It takes a significant amount of coordination to work all three control inputs smoothly— the collective (up and down), the cyclic (forward and back, left and right), and the pedals (nose rotation left and right)—and all three of these inputs affect the others. In a hover, for example, when you make an adjustment to the collective, you must also account for changes in balance and torque in the cyclic and pedals. It takes a lot of practice to hold a helicopter in a steady hover. Some people in our training program accomplished it quickly. I was not one of those people.

My instructor told me early on to set my focus on the horizon, but it didn't register. I kept staring down out at the ground directly in front of the helicopter, and then off to the side about twenty yards out, and then out front again. That caused me to be in a constant state of reaction, and most of the time my reactions were overcorrections. I then had to adjust to my overcorrections, and sometimes I reacted to those overcorrections with more overcorrections. It was a mess. It's similar to driving on the highway. If you focus your eyes on the road right in front of the car, you will constantly drift to the left or right. But if you set your focus further outward, toward the horizon, you can keep the car right in the center of the lane with only slight adjustments.

Most students hope to master the maneuver of hovering on the fourth or fifth flight. On my seventh flight, however, I finally allowed my focus to move outward to the tree line a few hundred yards ahead. And that's when it clicked. Everything was now in view. The ground in front of me was in view, the ground out to the side was in my periphery. I could immediately sense slight changes in the aircraft's movement—up, down, left, and right—and smartly adjust to them with relaxed control inputs. My hover was steady, and I gained great confidence in myself as a pilot in that moment. That confidence remained with me and helped me to make safe landings for the next four years aboard Navy warships in all kinds of seas, weather, and changing conditions. I had a presence of mind and an awareness of everything that was happening around me. I could process large amounts of information, including communications from air traffic controllers, notifications from other crew members, and all the data that the myriad of cockpit instruments displayed while controlling the aircraft smoothly. That awareness then allowed me to remain calm and present through all kinds of hectic and stressful circumstances. It enabled me to exercise good judgment in a dynamic and dangerous work environment. Most importantly, it enabled me to help serve all the people who counted on our helicopters to reach them.

Presence

Western culture is just starting to learn the power of presence, and there is a growing movement to embrace it. This movement is manifested in the growing popularity of meditation, yoga, psychological therapy, Eastern religions, and self-help.[1] Research also reveals that there are both mental and physical benefits associated with mindfulness and spiritual practices.[2] The military is learning about these benefits through commissioned studies.[3] Sectors of our health care system are discussing how to incorporate these practices into their treatment programs.[4] And areas of the corporate world are beginning to capitalize on them in their quest for efficiency and productivity.[5]

Do better, feel better, live better; of course, this trend is no accident in the twenty-first century. We have benefitted from technological advancements that alleviate physical discomforts, increase manufacturing efficiency, organize vast amounts of information, and provide lightning-fast means of communication. But these developments exist only in the physical realm. They do little to touch the depths of our humanity. New technologies might receive larger percentages of our attention today, but they are mostly empty and disconnected experiences for us as living, breathing, soulful humans.

The man at the center of the Christian religion was a huge proponent of connection to the present. It is one of the strongest messages flowing through Jesus' life and teachings. As Rob Bell said, "the way of Jesus is not about religion; it is about reality."[6] Reality *is* the present. It refers to events and circumstances happening right now. Jesus told people to pull their hearts, minds, and spirits into the present moment so they could live beautifully in their realities. Jesus worked to help people gain an understanding of their shallow, small-minded, selfish tendencies so they could work to overcome them. He wanted them to be aware of what was inside them—human nature, or sin—that always told them to shrink from their present challenges. And he wanted everyone he encountered, no matter their heritage or religion, to experience the richness of living in the present moment where he or she can connect with the source of all things: the Creator, whom he referred to as Father.

We rarely hear church leaders preach directly on the incredible freedom we experience in the pursuit of awareness and connection to the present, yet Jesus preached on it constantly. In Mark 13:33 he said to "stay alert." In Luke 21 he told people to "watch out" (Luke 21:34) and to "keep alert at all times" (Luke 21:36). In Matthew 13 Jesus said that people with eyes that cannot see and ears that do not hear won't understand his parables. In John 4:35 he told his disciples to "wake up and look around." In John 17:24, right before setting off to be tortured and killed, he prayed that his companions could "be with me where I am." And in Luke 23:34, one of his final sentences on the cross was a prayer for people who "don't know what they are doing."

We move in communion, like a symbiotic union, with God when we are connected to the present. And when we connect with the present, we connect with eternity. There might be no better way to describe it than divine and holy. Yet many church leaders overlook this basic, universal concept. Maybe that's because it's rarely been connected directly to traditional doctrine, church practices, or scholarly descriptions of the spiritual realm. But it's so important because it has everything to do with our lives, right now.

The pursuit of awareness and presence flows throughout the life that Jesus lived and the entire canon of his teachings. So why wouldn't people in the Christian faith today go all in with it? Jesus never asked anyone to construct buildings and hold worship services in his honor. He never asked people to sing to him. He never told anyone to write creeds, erect statues, or establish accredited degree programs based on his teachings. These are all man's devices.

Jesus overwhelmingly referred to himself as the Son of Man, a human, rather than the Son of God. He constantly directed praise and attention away from himself and redirected it toward God, his figurative Father (Matthew 11:27; John 5:24; 20:17). He was so intent on sharing his message that he would shout it out at crowds during festivals (John 7:37) and expound on it with the hordes of people following him around the countryside (Matthew 4:25; Luke 14:25; John 6:2). And he was constantly trying to avoid their exhausting adoration by escaping them (Matthew 5:1;13:36; Mark 6:32). Jesus was overwhelmingly not promoting himself. He was promoting a way of life—his way. And his *way* was focused on living with beauty, sincerity, awareness, and connection to God in every moment.

When I read the Gospels, I see Jesus constantly imploring people to let go of the past (Matthew 15:3); to love wholly both the familiar and unfamiliar people around them (Luke 10:36); to live joyfully right now (John 15:11); to throw parties when something good happens (Luke 15:9); to weep with people when something terrible happens (John 11:35); to cherish each opportunity to be generous (Matthew 6:19); to face injustice boldly alongside the oppressed (Matthew 5:11); to stand up for the weak (John 8:10); and to detach from our concerns over storing up our wealth and possessions as we learn to follow him (Mark 10:21). His example and teachings are a passionate urging for us to live beautifully in this present moment.

Not Death . . . Life

So often Christians celebrate Jesus' worth and accomplishments in abstract spiritual terms, or they promote his value as our grand rescuer from undesirable post-death circumstances. But throughout the Gospels Jesus' passion was acutely focused on showing us how to live beautifully in the present moment. He was showing us how to serve others and how to deal with challenges, hurt, pain, anger, jealousy, pride, oppression, and unfair treatment in ways that transcend smallness and self-centeredness. Jesus spoke about mind-sets and choices that result in lives that are full of deep, lasting joy (John 4:36). He made it clear that our choice to follow him can affect our lives in beautiful ways (John 8:12). A lot of Christians assume that Jesus came to warn us about spending the afterlife in some hot, torturous place. But overwhelmingly, he emphasized that our present circumstances have prime importance.

Even in Matthew 25, where Jesus spoke at length about metaphorical end-of-time concepts, the ultimate question he asked, the moral of the discussion, and the whole point of his rant was whether or not we will have spent our lives serving others. Did we feed people who were hungry? Did we give a drink to people who were thirsty? Did we invite strangers who were in need into our home? Did we give clothing to people who needed it? And did we visit people who were sick or in prison? He was speaking very pointedly about serving others in this lifetime.

What we do today matters! How we live matters! And the importance of it is crystal clear in Jesus' example and teachings. Brian McLaren made this startling point: "Most commonly, John's translation of Jesus' original phrase is rendered 'eternal life' in English. Unfortunately the phrase *eternal life* is often misinterpreted to mean 'life in heaven after you die.'"[7] McLaren continues, "The Greek phrase John uses for 'eternal life' literally means 'life of the ages.'"[8] And once we understand that the phrase "eternal life" has a metaphorical aspect, we understand that it's not necessarily about something that happens in the future.

The phrase "life of the ages" can help us see something that many of us might already know. The purpose of our faith is not to look forward to our death. It's to pour our efforts into this life! And when we acknowledge this, suddenly the impetus to thank God for saving us from some afterlife punishment evaporates. The weight that many of us carry from our insistence on avoiding some sort of eternal torture washes away. And suddenly we see the real value, relevance, and beauty in this Christian faith. It's no longer about transactions— just *believe* something so you can *get* a post-death reward. It's about this very moment and the manner in which we live.

Perhaps many Christians severely underestimate what they can experience on Earth. In Mark 9:1 Jesus said, "I tell you the truth, some standing here right now will not die before they see the Kingdom of God arrive in great power!" He's not telling us that we first die and then have this incredible experience. People will be alive when they have it!

In John 5:24 Jesus said, "Those who listen to my message and believe in God who sent me have eternal life. . . . They have already passed from death into life." In John 8:12 he said, "If you follow me, you won't have to walk in darkness, you will have the light that leads to life." And in Matthew 21:31 Jesus said, "Corrupt tax collectors and prostitutes will get into the Kingdom of God before you do." This is not a debate about who *dies* first. It's a matter of who decides to *live* first!

In Matthew 23 Jesus criticized the religious establishment because they were keeping others from understanding this concept and from entering heaven. He yelled at them, called them hypocrites, and chided them for not going in themselves. This was not a censure of any Pharisees who had died and then tried to skirt away from the so-called pearly gates. It was a rant against religious leaders who were choosing not to enter heaven every day of their lives.

Even the hallmark verse of modern Christianity, John 3:16—"For God so loved the world . . ."—is about living right now. Christians often assume this verse addresses the afterlife, implying a transactional reward that finds us after we die, but our hearts don't have to stop beating to get it. The verse does say that we "will not perish," but of course we'll die. This discussion is not about the *end* of our lives on earth. It's about *life* and *death* in a much more profound sense!

For many people, the point of the Christian faith is to avoid hell after they die. This is a real concern for many people in the Christian faith, but we must realize that Scripture is anything but clear on what hell is and if it even exists at all. Bible scholar Bart Ehrman said, "There is no place of eternal punishment in any passage of the entire Old Testament. In fact—and this comes as a surprise to many people —nowhere in the entire Hebrew Bible is there any discussion at all of heaven and hell as places of rewards and punishment for those who have died."[9] Similarly Bible scholar Peter Enns said, "There's no real clear notion of afterlife . . . in the Old Testament," and "the notion of being tormented for eternity . . . is utterly foreign to the New Testament."[10] Pastor and philosophy professor Jared Byas stated that the concept of the afterlife is simply "not central in the Bible" and that it "doesn't seem to be important to the biblical writers to get really clear on what happens when you die."[11] That's because, as both Enns and Byas point out, ancient Jews changed and developed their beliefs about the afterlife throughout the course of the Bible.[12] Ehrman has also explained that "The apostle Paul had different views of the afterlife from Jesus, whose views were not the same as those found in the Gospel of Luke or the Gospel of John or the book of Revelation."[13]

Bible scholar Meghan Henning revealed that a large number of Old Testament authors initially declared that the afterlife was a place where every person went, where not much happened, and where no one wanted to go. This wasn't because the destination was tortuous. People didn't want to go there simply because it meant they were dead. Their lives were over. Ehrman described it as a "complete diminution of life, to the point of virtual nonexistence."[14] Henning then points out that as Jewish culture began to mix with Greek and Roman culture, ideas on the afterlife mixed and morphed into concepts where different souls now went to different places, but the specifics were anything but clear. And when Jesus used language of the afterlife he was overwhelmingly making points about the manner in which people lived. Henning said that Jesus spoke about the after-life in the "contexts of ethical construction."[15] He was making points about the ethics of people's lives—their choices and behaviors. Henning said that Jesus and other New Testament authors were "using this [afterlife] language to try to persuade audiences to behave in particular ways."[16] And *behavior* has everything to do with the present moment. So perhaps we often miss the point when we emphasize heaven and hell as post-death concepts. And perhaps we severely underestimate what we can experience today!

Look at your life today. Is it perfect? Is joy present? Hopefully some amount of joy is present in your life. But is there also anxiety, anger, resentment, shame, depression, and loneliness? Is any of that a burden? Does that stuff ever make you feel empty and awful? It sure sounds a lot like what Jesus described when he spoke of "weeping and gnashing of teeth" in Luke 13:28. And the suffering and torment that we experience when we take our lives in ugly, selfish directions —that experience might even be what he was referring to when he spoke of "the never-ending fire" in Matthew 3:12. Perhaps that *is* hell!

Father Richard Rohr also explained that the concept of hell, or death, is something that we experience today. He said very plainly, "You can choose death now."[17] And shouldn't the knowledge of this choice wake us up to a startling reality, that sometimes we experience hell because *we* choose it? Sometimes our lives are filled with turmoil because we fail to choose thoughts, actions, and behaviors that are life-giving. Perhaps this is why we often live in anxiety, anger, resentment, shame, depression, and loneliness. So maybe it's time to start talking about how we can become better at *choosing* life? And maybe we need to do this right away! As Father Rohr said, "It really is urgent now."[18] He added, "If we don't get this clarified for history, I'm not sure how the Christian message... [is ever] going to make sense to much of the world. It's not going to be 'good news to all the world'" (Luke 2:10).[19] Perhaps for many of us, that is already the case.

If you have assumed that getting a ticket to some mystical heavenly experience after we die is more important than living in a *heavenly* manner now, I urge you to read the Gospels again. Learn from Jesus' life. See what he really was teaching and the behaviors that he was exhibiting. See how he was keenly focused on the present moment and being wholly *present* in it. Brian McLaren said that the person who participates "in the healing of the world is very different" from the person who prefers to leave this world and "go to a better one."[20] People who are waiting around for things to get fixed, or waiting around to die, will have very little impact. They have very little reason to bring good things into the world. And they may never conceive of the beautiful and profound things that can happen in their lives today. That person's circumstances sound like a life in darkness, or hell, or death. But Jesus explained a clear way out of it. In John 8:12 he said, "If you follow me"—follow in his way—"you won't have to walk in darkness."

Jesus gave us an understanding of how to move beyond anxiety, anger, resentment, shame, and depression. He taught us how to move into the present moment, where we can experience clarity and beauty, and where we can have a profound impact on the world around us. And maybe in the twenty-first century this can become our understanding of eternal life, the "life of the ages," or as Father Rohr says, "ultimate life."[21] This could really make our faith relevant and cause it to matter today. Isn't it worth investigating?

9. THE WAY

A few years ago I had a discussion with a friend about church. We had both been lifelong churchgoers, but I told him I was thinking about not going anymore, that I was just losing interest. He expressed a similar feeling. He said, "You know, I went Sunday to our church, and it was another letdown. I just didn't learn anything." I knew exactly what he was feeling, but I couldn't completely articulate why. The Bible-based sermons I was hearing were new to my ears, but they still felt stale.

Then shortly after that I heard a woman who is often on the national news speak about her faith and the different churches she has attended. She said one thing that really caught my attention. She was asked if she reads the Bible. She replied by explaining that she does read it occasionally, but mostly just the Gospels, the books that account for Jesus' life. As for the rest of the Bible she said, "No, because, like, I got it. I know what it says."

I was kind of alarmed when I heard her say this. I thought, "How dare she say that she *knows* what's in the Bible. How dare anyone assume that they've just *got it*." But the more I thought about her comments, the more I understood them. And I realized that my experience was similar. I couldn't get enough of reading the Gospels. I found so much good, tangible stuff that related directly to my life. I loved reading Jesus' teachings about life and love and inclusion and overcoming the smallness of both our culture and our human nature. There was such perfection in it. But I was also becoming bored with a lot of other elements of the church experience.

Sermons on Old Testament stories were still being advertised as important simply because they came from the Bible, not because they moved in our lives. Preachers were still proclaiming, in case I missed it the first hundred times, that Jesus was Lord and that all my sins were forgiven. The repetitive adoration of Jesus in praise music was starting to feel elementary, both spiritually and intellectually. And the incessant moral instruction from preachers who had no higher moral standing than I was just getting tiresome. Church wasn't bad. In fact, it was mostly good, but it was getting boring. I'd heard it all before. Many times. I *got it*.

Moving Beyond Beliefs

The Barna Group says that church attendance dropped steadily from 45 percent to 25 percent between 2000 and 2020.[1] And from what I hear from church leaders today, social distancing does anything but help to boost those numbers. To me it's clear that vast numbers of people just don't find the message of the church useful or relevant. I see evidence in the statistics, and I've heard this sentiment expressed from more people than I can remember. There are many reasons why the message of the church doesn't connect with people's lives, but sometimes I wonder if a large number of people simply outgrew it. From countless conversations that I've had, it appears that most people didn't give up on their beliefs. They didn't toss their faith in the trash, but they may have put it on the shelf.

This makes me wonder if the version of faith many people are handed by their churches is just too simplistic, too sedentary, and too small. And therefore it can't grow into their lives, and it can't become relevant. This was certainly the case for me. Church services were fine for an hour on Sunday, but they didn't have much to say about how the rest of my week would go. And many of the services I attended were self-perpetuating, thus affirming their increasing insignificance. We would do things, say things, and sing things just so we could keep doing and saying and singing them the next week. But I often wondered, what else is there?

Follow

In his book *Falling Upward*, Father Richard Rohr relates our spiritual development to philosopher Carl Jung's concept of the "two halves of life." Jung wrote extensively on this topic, and Rohr offered one statement from Jung that attempts to sum it up: "One cannot live the afternoon of one's life according to the program of life's morning, for what was great in the morning will be of little importance in the evening, and what in the morning was true will at evening become a lie."[2]

There is room to separate our faith experience from the exact words of Jung's quote here, but the larger message should not be ignored. At some point many of us move on from the simplistic, repetitive acts of passive Bible reading, praising God, and reminding ourselves that we believe something. Father Rohr said, "All this worshipping of Jesus . . . I know you've got to do it in the first half of life to find your focus. You need devotion. You need to fall to your knees. . . . to say 'You are my Lord and my teacher.' But then we don't really let him *be* our teacher. We just keep worshiping the icon."[3]

Not everyone moves into a *second half* of faith. Some people choose not to. Some lack the ability. And unfortunately, some never do because their church fails to lead them there.

Acclaimed Christian author Philip Yancey asked this question: "What does the world learn about God by watching its followers on earth?"[4] This is a terribly important question today, especially as we consider how the Christian church at large has struggled to attract people to its services, much less keep the remaining people in its pews. Another good question for Christ followers is, What would Christ learn about us from watching us? Would he be happy that we internalize his legacy? Would he commend us for believing that he was God incarnate? And would he be satisfied that we express adoration toward him?

The more I read the Gospels, the more clear it is that Jesus' primary intent was not to have people worship him. Instead he wanted people to take notice of his *way*, and to follow it. In John 8:12 he said, "If you follow me, you won't have to walk in darkness." In Matthew 19:21 he said, "If you want to be perfect, go and sell all your possessions and give the money to the poor, and you will have treasure in heaven. Then come, follow me." And upon first meeting two of his disciples, Peter and Andrew, who were fisherman, he said, "Come, follow me, and I will show you how to fish for people!" (Matthew 4:19). Jesus also implored people to follow him in Matthew 9:9 and 16:24, Mark 2:14, Luke 5:27 and 18:22, and in John 1:43, 8:12, and 21:19. These were not pleas for people to stop and bow prostrate. They were not calls to genuflect. They were calls to follow his *way*. Maybe that's because his *way* really does offer something profound for our lives.

For many of us, the word faith is a passive word. It refers to concepts that we accept to be true. It's wonderful to embrace good and godly concepts, but what does that really say about us? Does it change anything in our lives? Father Rohr said that in the modern Christian tradition, so often "we worship the messenger instead of the message. . . . We worship Jesus as an icon of specialness and absolute uniqueness instead of following him. And it's very clear in all four Gospels he said 'follow me.' He did not say 'worship me.' In John's gospel he says 'what I have done you also must do.' That's a significant change of position, of strategy, if we can see Jesus as the model. . . the mentor of what union looks like, what union feels like, and what we also can do."[5] Rohr was referring to Jesus' words in John 13:15: "I have given you an example to follow. Do as I have done to you." That sounds a lot more like following than genuflecting.

Jesus also said, "I am the way, the truth, and the life. No none comes to the Father except through me" (John 14:6). But does that mean we have to keep telling Jesus how great he is so we can "get to" the Father? Or does that mean when we follow his way, his truth, and his life. . . *that* is when we experience God in us? Jesus also said to *believe* in him many times. But what if the *belief* that he mentioned is more closely tied to following him, trusting his way, and embodying his teachings than just accepting him as a reality?

Trust in the Way

There is one question that doesn't get asked enough in the Christian faith today. It's short and simple, and it might provide insight into why the message of the church fails to connect with a lot of people. That question is, So what?

Many people in the Christian faith were taught that the story of their faith ends when they just believe something. If they just accept who Jesus was and what he did, and then bow down in worship, then their spiritual work is finished. At that point everything is resolved. They can die and God will let them into some ethereal paradise. But when we really take notice of Jesus' teachings on heaven and eternal life, we understand that he wasn't solely talking about events that happen after our death. He was also talking about our lives today. Right now. So new questions must then be asked.

So what if we have faith? *So what* if God is great? *So what* if we believe that Jesus died and rose from the dead? *So what* if our sins are forgiven? And what we're really saying when we ask these questions is, What happens now? Does any of this matter? Is any of this relevant in our lives?

Perhaps many people misunderstand what Jesus said about beliefs. The English word *belief* can simply mean to accept something as true, to agree to its rightness. In this case it's practically intellectual, and therefore it's passive. And that makes Jesus' words in John 3:16 pretty simplistic: "everyone who believes in him will . . . have eternal life." But *pisteuo*, the Greek word from which *belief* was translated, means so much more than a passive agreement. It also means to trust. And our trust comes alive only when we are willing to embody it. We truly trust something when we are willing to base our actions on it, to risk something for it. We really trust something when we start following it. That's when our beliefs become significant in our lives. Sometimes we might get mocked or persecuted because of this trust, but we also know that it's good to keep trusting and keep following, at the next step and the one after that. That's when the *way* of Christ can really affect our lives, our relationships, and our communities.

Perhaps in John 3:16 Jesus was telling people not to be passive but to *show* in their actions that they trust his way, knowing that it will lead to good things. Maybe embodying Jesus' life and teachings is actually the "truth" that will "set us free" from all kinds of ugliness and suffering (John 8:32). Maybe in Mark 9:23 when Jesus said that "anything is possible if a person believes," he was saying that many good things are possible in our lives when we follow his *way*. And maybe in John 5:24 when he said, "Those who listen to my message and believe in God who sent me have eternal life," he's telling us that we can have a beautiful, impactful, and profound life when we follow his *way*, which is the *way* of God, our unfathomable Creator who brought us into this earth out of love.

My favorite story about Christ is in John 7. In the middle of a festival, Jesus stood and shouted at the crowds, "Anyone who is thirsty may come to me! Anyone who believes in me may come and drink! For the Scriptures declare, 'Rivers of living water flow from his heart'" (John 7:37–38). The writer of John then explains that he was talking about the Spirit of God being in us and flowing from us, like a union between God and our hearts. And this is when we experience God's incredible *life*. This *life* and all its goodness will flow from us. Jesus didn't declare that he would rescue us from anything. Jesus didn't say that he would dump buckets of living water onto our heads to cleanse us or fix us. Nor was he telling us to passively accept his existence as reality. He was talking about our lives and what comes from them when we trust his *way*!

Now consider a flowing river. A flowing river doesn't flow occasionally. A flowing river doesn't flow only during those times when we obey religious laws. Nor does it only flow during a church service. A flowing river just keeps flowing. It constantly gushes forth, overwhelming us with incredible life experience—beautiful, fulfilling, *eternal* life. This is possible when we come to him, his life, his *way*, and we commit to it.

Do you grasp how profound this is? And do you grasp how different this could be from the self-centered, anxious, day-to-day approach to life that we are accustomed to in the twenty-first century? A life of flowing beauty, peace, love, and meaning is ours if we choose it! And if we make a practice of choosing this way of life, it can become ours in every moment and every changing circumstance.

If you're looking for something more for your life—a way to move beyond all the smallness, superficiality, shallowness, and emptiness that we are constantly immersed in—then consider following Jesus' *way*. Consider putting your trust in it. Consider believing that it will bring good things into your life. If you don't know much about his *way* and the incredible *life* that it offers, keep reading this book, but also consider reading through the Gospels. These are the first four books in the New Testament: Matthew, Mark, Luke, and John. It's the account of Jesus' life by those four disciples. Gain an understanding of the context: ancient Jewish culture that was overtaken by Roman imperialism and small-minded religious authorities. Look at what Jesus said and how he lived. Look at the joy he brought to people. Look at how he respected and loved people. Look at how he touched and healed them. Look at the authenticity and goodness that he brought to discussions about spirituality, politics, religion, relationships, racial tension, and humanity's never-ending obsession with wealth and social status. Look at the connection he had with the divine and how it was directed at circumstances here on earth, in people's lives. And pay close attention when he insists that there is a better *way*. Because there is. His *way*. It works. It's nothing but good. It's impactful and profound. It's practical and relevant. This *way* is our extraordinary opportunity to live better in the twenty-first century.

Union

In my life of faith I have found that the next step, beyond beliefs and simple worship, is to live every day connected to God. Another way to describe it is a union with God. And isn't a union with God, whether it be a deep and prayerful experience or just a constant mindfulness about our thoughts and actions, something that could really affect us? Couldn't that make our faith come alive and allow it to become present in our lives? Isn't that what so many of us want? And if it is, isn't that where we should focus our energies?

This isn't a rejection or even a diminishing of our love for Christ or of our unfathomable Creator. It's the opposite. It builds on it! It's the embodiment of it. It's the ultimate manifestation of our foundational love, adoration, and respect for God.

Jesus was the perfect example of union. He was both human and divine, and he implored us to be the same. In John 10:30 he said, "The Father and I are one." And in John 14:20 he said, "When I am raised to life again, you will know that I am in my Father, and you are in me, and I am in you." And perhaps this was Jesus' message about the rituals of baptism and the eucharist, or communion, as Protestants call it: "eat" his body and "drink" his blood. This practice helps us commune with God, becoming one in heart, mind, and spirit.

Paul, the author of more than half of the New Testament books, capitalized on this concept. He said in 1 Corinthians 6:17, "The person who is joined to the Lord is one spirit with him." Then in 1 Corinthians 3:16 he said, "Don't you realize that all of you together are the temple of God and that the Spirit of God lives in you?"

The concept of union, embodiment, and communion could really turn some heads in the Christian church today. It could raise some eyebrows because it has an entirely different set of ramifications than passively bowing down in worship, pleading to be rescued, and looking forward to events that happen after we die. The concept of union is a tricky thing for many Christians, because it's often easier to keep our distance. It's less intrusive and it takes less effort when we remain separated from the divine. We hardly have to move a muscle when we just point up to heaven in worship. And when we do that, we often emphasize our distance from God. We declare that God is up there, and we lowly people are down here. This kind of mind-set is not union. It's separation. And in this mind-set, we can develop an addiction for worship, recognition, and adoration because we are forced to constantly plead to God for mercy. In our insistence on distance from the divine, we constantly feel a need for God to rescue us from all the pitiful circumstances that we're stuck in. This is not union and *life*; it's self-pity.

I wonder if some people today look at the Christian experience as insane—go to the same church and participate in the same Bible-based worship service every week and expect that things will change. Isn't that the definition of insanity? But if union is both the purpose and the reward, then our lives can really transform. We can invite and receive all kinds of beauty, depth and meaning. The incredible heart of our Creator can move into our lives, even into places that we thought were lost to darkness.

Perhaps this aspect of the Christian faith has been missing for many people because their churches focus so heavily on genuflecting toward God—reminding both ourselves and God, over and over again, who and where each partner is in the relationship. This simple awareness can be an important step in people's faith, but when do they move past it? When are they ready for the next step in their personal and spiritual maturity? The Christian church spends immense amounts of time, effort, and resources on worship services —their recognition of, submission to, and adoration before God. Week after week, churches hold worship services where people declare that "God is great." But at some point, don't we *get it*, like the woman I heard interviewed who had grown bored with Old Testament stories? And aren't we ready for something more, like my friend who wasn't *learning* anything in church?

Perhaps once again we should look to the man at the center of the Christian religion, and take seriously his plea to follow him. Jesus spoke about the greatness of God often, but he also spent his life teaching about a profound way to live connected to it. He talked about the work that needs to be done to experience an *eternal* kind of life that's based in goodness and union with God. And he was the ultimate example of it. It's a fascinating prospect, and I wonder how many bored Christians, former churchgoers, and even skeptical nonbelievers might find it worthy of investigating today.

10. THE SYMBOL

Thomas Edison once said, "What you are will show in what you do." I certainly keep learning that lesson in my life. It's true in my work, my neighborhood, my friendships, my parenting, and my marriage. I want to be someone good. I want to embody and manifest good things, just like the *way* of Jesus. His *way* was perfect. Unblemished, beautiful, impactful, and profound. It doesn't sound petty, self-centered, superficial, or shallow. It doesn't sound like it will lead me to the same old short-sighted, disconnected, and sometimes harmful *ways* that I often choose. It also sounds like his *way* could do a lot of good in my life and in the lives of the people around me. I want that kind of life, because it sounds awesome. It sounds like a lot of good things can be present in my life when I subscribe to it. Not necessarily financial success or improved looks or fast cures from illnesses, but good thoughts, good relationships, true peace, and deep joy. And certainly, if I am living that kind of life, it will get noticed. Regardless of anyone's understanding of the Bible, they will know that the *way* of my life comes from someplace good.

The second chapter of the book of James contains a section that has a lot to say about the *way* of Jesus, and it contains some harsh language for people who didn't understand just how transforma-

tional it could be. In verse 14 James begins a rant about the focus of
his listeners. Apparently these people were quite proud of their faith.
They must have held it in high regard, but there must not have been
much in their lives to show for it. So James criticized them for being
misguided and small-minded. He said in verse 17, "So you see, faith
by itself isn't enough. Unless it produces good deeds, it is dead and
useless." Then he turned up the heat a notch and mocked them with
sarcasm: "You say you have faith, for you believe that there is one
God. Good for you! Even demons believe this, and they tremble in
terror" (James 2:19). And then he laid into them: "How foolish! Can't
you see that faith without good deeds is useless?" (James 2:20).

Useless without good deeds, said James. Not holy. Not righteous.
Not God-pleasing. And not just insignificant, but utterly *useless*—
useless to people, useless to the world, and useless for God. And by
good deeds, of course, James wasn't referring to favors that people
occasionally do for others. He was referring to the manner in which
they lived among each other, the way their faith manifested in their
lives, and the way it touched others. Perhaps James is emphatic here
because his audience was doing very little to embody their faith.
Perhaps their faith hadn't moved beyond their beliefs and into any
kind of union with God. James doesn't even mention whether or not
they spent considerable time worshipping God. That activity apparently had very little significance in the discussion. The issue was
much larger than beliefs, convictions, and worship—all the things
that a lot of churches today love to emphasize. The issue was with
their lives—who they are and what they do.

For me and for a massive and growing population in our culture,
living well and doing good things for this world is important. And as
James pointed out, that's what matters. That's when our faith can
affect us. That's when it impacts the world around us. Like James
pointed out about Jesus' life in verse 22, that's when it becomes
"complete."

Good News

The Christian church does an enormous amount of good in the world. These efforts are not in question, and they certainly are a manifestation of people's faith. Understand also that the Christian church at large is thriving in many parts of the world. Africa, for example, has been experiencing a boom in church growth for many years now.[1] But in Western Christian culture, we must ask why there is such a disconnect between the message that the church at large preaches and people's regard for it. Perhaps one reason is because the church has not helped enough people become something better and experience real goodness in their everyday lives. Perhaps, because there has been such an emphasis on believing the right things and bowing down before God, people realized that the church wasn't really interested in them. Perhaps people really do hear the message of the church and how it keeps God on high and people down low.

If a message of lowliness has been emphasized in your life, I invite you right now to consider another idea—that you might actually be amazing. You are God's unique creation. There is no one like you. Your physical, mental, and emotional presence is not like anyone else's. Anywhere. And please don't ever think that your uniqueness is not significant. Because no one else can affect the world the way that you can. Your talents, your skills, your beliefs, your passions—they are ready to be put to good use.

Please don't ever convince yourself that you can't bring goodness into the world in your unique way. Please don't believe that you can't be a positive influence in your world, however small that world may be. Please don't think that you don't have a God-given opportunity to affect the course of your life and the lives of others. And please don't convince yourself that this moment does not matter, that it can pass by without care, and that Jesus will fix everything later. You are capable of doing so much good now! You can bring such beauty into the world! You can have such great impact! You have an opportunity to influence the world around you at every moment. Jesus even said that you can move mountains (Matthew 17:20)! How ridiculously empowering is that?!

Rob Bell, an accomplished Bible scholar, said that he "can't find one place in the teachings of Jesus, or the Bible for that matter, where we are to identify ourselves first and foremost as sinners."[2] Of course, smallness, sinfulness, and lowliness are part of our existence, but they do not define our totality. Yes, we are sinners. Yes, we are limited in the good that we can do by our human nature. But we are also God's incredible creation. If you need the Bible to tell you this, then be assured that it says and over just how valuable we are to our Creator. The first book of the Bible even says that we were created in God's image, or likeness. And, as Jesus said in Matthew 22:37–40, the Greatest Commandment is to love God and our neighbor. And how do we show love? How do we impact the world around us in a manner that is in union with the Creator of the universe? By doing good for people, for ourselves, and the world around us.

What You Do

The good things that you *do* matter! In Matthew 25:40, after describing all kinds of beautiful things we can do for others, Jesus said, "When you did it to one of the least of these my brothers and sisters, you were doing it to me" In that phrase, the most important word is the verb—the forms of the word *do*. And as the apostle John said, "anyone who does what pleases God will live forever" (1 John 2:17).

Paul, who is often associated with the message of total reliance on Jesus, lived a difficult life. But does anyone think that Paul was lying around helplessly in his prison cell, not willing to move a muscle in self-preservation? Does anyone really think that he was not willing to use his God-given mental capacities to transcend his conditions? Did he give up all hope for survival and just hand the situation over for Jesus to operate? Did he become a lifeless puppet? If you think Paul was telling us to give up our human autonomy and passively believe something, please read his letters again. This time understand that he was extremely headstrong and determined. He made the choice to live in strength and defiance of abusive authorities. He even said it himself, "I can do everything through Christ, who gives me strength" (Philippians 4:13). He didn't say that Christ would do all things *for* him. He said *he* could do them when he lived in union with God.

And if Paul exhibited any behavior deserving of sainthood, it was his insistence on *doing* things that lead to a beautiful, impactful, and profound life. He wrote about it in every one of his letters. Embrace the present. Follow the perfect example of Jesus. Know his life and teachings. Stop fooling around with self-centered activities that lead to feelings of emptiness. Raise each other up. Stand firm in your deepest beliefs. Look out for people who need help and lend a generous hand to them. Work through petty arguments that disconnect you from others. Stop putting feckless idols and empty philosophies on pedestals. Know the dangers of assuming that other people's philosophies, doctrines, and practices hold all the answers for you. Don't be burdened by strict religiosity. And don't waste a second before doing all of this. Do it today!

Two Bible scholars, Sylvia Keesmaat and Bryan Walsh, studied the original Greek text of the book of Romans, Paul's letter to a small group of people in Rome. The book of Romans is often upheld as a source to understand systematic theology—all the abstract stuff about God and the spiritual realm. But Keesmaat and Walsh found that Paul was overwhelmingly trying to help people in Rome form beautiful and loving communities. They explain that Paul was less often expounding upon abstract spiritual concepts and more often teaching people how to defy Roman imperialistic culture—violence, exclusion, and oppression.[3] Paul's teachings were often set in the context of ancient Jewish religious topics, because through this he could show people what to do, how to act, how to live, how to transcend imperialistic behaviors and emulate the incredible *way* of Jesus.

Let's be very clear: this discussion is not about us becoming a superhero or something even more outrageous—perfect. We are neither perfect in our actions nor our beliefs. We never will be. Any pressure you feel to be perfect can be dropped right now. But also know that you can be so much more than you are today because there is so much more that you can *do*. Rob Bell said this: "Notice how many places in the accounts of Jesus' life he gets frustrated with his disciples. Because they are incapable? No, because of how capable they are. He sees what they could be and what they could do, and when they fall short, it provokes him to no end. It isn't the failure that's the problem; it's their greatness. They don't realize what they are capable of."[4]

We in the Christian faith undersell ourselves far too often. It's a healthy practice to accept that we are imperfect, but it's also a life-giving message to preach that we are capable! And perhaps Christian leaders don't preach that enough. Perhaps our culture has even taken notice, and that's one reason why the church so often fails to keep people's attention. In the twenty-first century, with all of our discon-nectedness and all the mental health challenges facing us, it can be problematic when the church preaches a message of human help-lessness and insignificance. Because when we constantly tell people that they need to worship Jesus to receive forgiveness, we essentially tell them that they're no good. When we constantly remind people that they should repent, we emphasize their faults. And when we advertise that people should simply *believe* something so they can *get* something in return (after they die), we tell them that their lives don't matter. This is not an issue of denying the reality of our shortcom-ings. It's a matter of putting it in balance. And for the Christian church at large today, the balance needs to shift toward empowering people and teaching them to live beautiful, impactful, and profound lives in union with our Creator.

The Cross

The symbol of Christianity is the cross. It's what we place atop our church buildings, print on bumper stickers, and display on our websites. It's a great symbol, and it's a metaphor for so many profound concepts. But it can also be a symbol of how and where our faith exists. Consider the four points of the cross: we look *up* to the heavens as we worship God, but we also look *down* to our lives and this incredible creation, and we look to our *left* and *right* to see what we can do to affect the people around us in good and loving ways.

Today the church is adept at worshipping God. It's been the focus for decades in our modern churches, and so praise music, worshipful sermons, and standing in awe of God has become common practice. At this point, we've knocked it out of the park. We've practically perfected it. I don't know what else many churches could do to improve this activity, especially the ones that have upgraded to concert PA systems, professional stage lighting, charismatic pastors, talented singers, and industry-level video productions. What else can they do in their adoration and worship of God? Maybe just turn the volume up so God can hear them better? I wonder sometimes, if Christians don't push their focus beyond adoration and worship, will they ever do enough good in the world to be noticed again? Will they ever reveal to the world that the message of Christ is a great option today?

Our culture is crying out. People everywhere are in need of connectedness and community. People all around us are battling darkness and depression. People everywhere need encouragement to keep moving forward in their lives. So many people need physical and financial help just to maintain basic, acceptable living conditions. So many people lack food, drinkable water, shelter from the elements—the things that most Americans take for granted. So many people need their spirits to be raised as they suffer from illness. So many people are hurting because of choices that fail to bring goodness into their lives. People are starving for something meaningful and powerful in their lives, something that can help them transcend the pains, frustrations, anxieties, and uncertainties of living in the twenty-first century. And we're putting our time and effort into worship services? Worship can be wonderful, but perhaps a vast number of people in our population need something more.

Maybe this understanding of the symbol of the cross is the church's best hope to have a positive impact in the world and to expand the incredible experience of Christ, to illuminate his *way*. Perhaps that's where our focus should be now and always: up toward God, but also down to our lives and this incredible creation, and out to the right and left, where so much work needs to be done. Just think of the good that we could do both in our personal lives and in our communities. Our world could really change. We really could move mountains.

11. TRUTH

I heard a joke once. It made me laugh because it poked fun at me and things I often do. That is, my tendency to believe sometimes that my faith has been completely figured out; that it's righteous and resolved.

> The devil and one of his new pupils were sitting on top of a building watching a man who was about to become a Christian.
>
> The pupil was concerned. "He's getting closer," he said. The man was just about to give his life to Jesus.
>
> The devil said calmly, "Don't worry. Just watch."
>
> The man got down on his knees. The pupil said worriedly, "We have to do something. We're about to lose him!"
>
> Just then the man stretched out his arms, closed his eyes, cried out to Jesus, and committed his life to his newfound Christian faith!
>
> The pupil was so upset. He looked up at the devil and asked, "Why didn't we stop him?"
>
> The devil patted him on the back and said, "Don't worry. We'll help him organize it later."

I've told this joke to several Christians. Most of them laughed, but some didn't appreciate it. It exposes a raw truth about the tendency in the Christian faith to expend exhaustive efforts trying to understand every detail about spirituality and theology. It pokes fun at our obsession with being right about biblical conclusions and interpretations. So it reminds us that there is more to life than getting every tedious detail out of Scripture. As the great Christian philosopher, St. Thomas Aquinas, said, "Prius vita qua doctrina," meaning "life is more important than doctrine."[1] Our lives need so much more than scholarly conclusions on Scripture. Not everything in our lives can be resolved and perfected. We are human *beings,* not human answers, interpretations, or conclusions. What matters sometimes more than perfect answers for our faith is the manner in which we seek them: based in goodness and always with an eye for truth.

Seek

There is a debate today in our culture regarding the definition of truth. The debate exists in part because different people can look at a topic and come away with completely different conclusions. And of course this is no surprise. Our conclusions are based on our perspectives, and our perspectives are largely determined by our disposition, education and experiences—all of which are unique for every single person. Even if we receive the same information on a topic, such as current events, politics, philosophy, or religion, people can make completely different conclusions. This often frustrates people. Some people are impatient to have their debates resolved, once and for all. They want everyone to agree on truth. But what that often means is that they want others to accept their perspective and their version of truth.

The word *seeker* is used a lot today to describe people who are searching for truth. It's often attributed to people who express an interest in spirituality, religious practices, or a system for living. For me this word is a little underwhelming because it doesn't describe just one type of person; it describes everyone. Whether people are conscious of it or not, every person is seeking a *right* way to live. Every human is seeking answers for their needs, desires, and questions. People just search in different places. People seek answers in their work, community, relationships, therapy, food, drink, chemicals, exercise, sex, hobbies, education, entertainment, as well as the spiritual realm. And all these things that we seek—answers for our needs, desires, and questions—are truth.

Humans are created with a need for truth. Animals are not created with this need. The mere existence of an animal *is* truth. Animals seem to know exactly what they are, what they are to do, and how they are to do it. Moral, ethical, and existential questions appear to be absent from the life of animals. They don't stop to consider if they are pursuing a solution to their needs in the *right* manner. They just pursue it. Humans, on the other hand, have an inherent compulsion to know that we are making the right decisions. We agonize over what words will come out of our mouths, what foods we will eat, what jobs we will take, what education to pursue, what route to drive, what home to live in, etc. And in every case, we must decide what the *right* choice is. This is our constant challenge: to live the right way and to seek truth for our lives.

Dualistic Thinking

As kids, we were taught that dualistic, or binary thinking, leads us to the *right* truths. It helped us identify *right* choices. We were taught to break down issues into two clear options by finding or fabricating a line through them. It allowed us to avoid complexity, nuance, and contradiction. We pushed all the resolvable stuff to one side and the unresolvable stuff to another. It was a matter of reorganizing complicated issues into simplistic forms. Naturally, then, we identified with the resolvable side, and that allowed us to identify our opposition on the other side.

Children cannot comprehend an issue that is filled with complexity, nuance, and contradiction, nor should they. Children need simplicity. Their minds are not mature. They have not developed. For a child, every learning opportunity must be presented in a simplified form. So naturally, parents and teachers divide each issue into two clear sides. For example, don't ever steal, don't ever lie, and don't ever eat a cookie before dinner. *Good* behavior must be easily identifiable, as must *bad* behavior. Of course, as adults there are deeper considerations to these rules. We might see it as perfectly acceptable to borrow office supplies from a coworker without giving them notice. We might see value in hiding the knowledge of a surprise birthday party from someone. And many of us can eat a cookie before dinner without guilt or consequence.

The world of adulthood contains complexity, nuance, and contradiction. The world of a child does not. Children must first learn the importance of following rules before they can decide which rules to follow. They need this skill to function and fit into familial, educational, and communal systems. It helps them learn their community's definition of *right* behavior, so it helps them survive and stay out of trouble. Dualistic thinking was useful for us as children. But we are no longer children.

Father Richard Rohr has spoken about dualistic thinking often. He provides great insight into the need for those of us in the Christian faith to move beyond it. He said, "Dualistic or divided people live in a split and fragmented world. They cannot accept that God objectively dwells within them or others (1 Cor 3:16–17). They cannot accept or forgive certain parts of themselves. This lack of forgiveness takes the form of a tortured mind, a closed heart, or an inability to live calmly and humbly inside their own body. The fragmented mind sees parts, not wholes, and invariably it creates antagonism, fear, and resistance."[2]

You will identify dualistic thinking in more places in your life once you become aware of it. It is pervasive in our culture, especially in our politics. So many people who choose one side of a political issue often then turn to the other side and commence the spewing of ridicule, accusation, and insult. This is what Father Rohr called the "fragmented mind." It's difficult to face complexity, nuance, and contradiction, so often we just avoid it by splitting our political, ethical, and theological issues into simplistic halves. This behavior resembles the mind-sets that we were taught to embrace as children —young and immature children. But at some point we should no longer act, think, and reason like children. We must mature beyond dualistic thinking and enter nondualistic thinking if we are to grow as adults, and grow in our faith.

Contradiction

It's a profound experience to accept ourselves, finally, as whole beings, with both positive and negative qualities. It's humbling to stand before another person and ask them to accept us, with all our good, our bad, and our ugly. But we can mature to the point where we hold these positive and negative qualities together in tension, and the acceptance of this tension can bring us profound peace.

It's also a profound experience when we finally learn that other people hold contradictions, that each person on this planet exhibits both helpful and harmful behavior. Of course, it's easy to say that we *hate* people when they exhibit harmful behavior, just like it's easy to say that we *like* people when they display helpful behavior. But when we *hate* someone, we reduce that person to only those qualities and moments that we dislike. And often times when we *like* someone, we reduce their existence to just those moments that make us feel good. In both cases, these are not complete and accurate representations of people. They are limited, inadequate, and immature ways of defining them.

We are both positive and negative; we are both immaculate and unclean; we are both good and evil. Pete Rollins, an author and philosopher who often speaks about the Christian experience in our modern culture, said that "we are between life and death. We are being and nothing-ness. . . . We are a contradiction."[3] Rollins also shared that the nineteenth-century philosopher Martin Heidegger said that one great contradiction humans have is that they don't know how to be human.[4] We are always searching and working to figure out what it means to be the best version of ourselves. This might seem confusing or discouraging at first glance, but it's how God created us. We are not simple creatures. We are not entirely resolvable, nor is the world around us. This might be why we have so many questions about truth. Deepak Chopra gives us this insightful explanation:

> The self is divided. Again there are many expressions of this inescapable fact, but they generally play on the notion of opposites. Humans are divine and animal in their nature, capable of the highest good and the worst evil, driven by the conscious and the unconscious. So thoroughly is the divided self embedded in the rise of homo sapiens that we possess a higher and lower brain, feeling torn between reason and irrational drives for sex, survival, and perhaps love and hate.[5]

It can be a scary thing to accept someone who exhibits behavior that we hate. Contrarily, it can be terribly painful to learn that someone we love has harmed us. It also can be a strenuous process to accept ourselves, with all of our faults and shortcomings. For most of us, the process takes years. And for some of us it takes a lifetime. But we are capable. We can grow in spite of the unresolved questions about ourselves, our world, and our faith.

Nonviolent protest, the method that Dr. Martin Luther King, Jr. promoted for social justice, was a difficult concept for people to embrace at first. It was a total contradiction—a paradox. It's built on the premise of loving our enemies—showing grace to people who don't extend grace toward us. But Dr. King made it clear that we must accept contradiction if we are to be strong, impactful people. He said, "The strong man holds in a living blend strongly marked opposites. Not ordinarily do men achieve this balance of opposites. The idealists are not usually realistic, and the realists are not usually idealistic. The militant are generally not known to be passive, nor the passive to be militant. Seldom are the humble self-assertive. Or the self-assertive humble."[6] None of these attributes are in themselves bad qualities. But when any one of them is singular in our lives, when we feel a need to run to one side or the other, we can quickly find ourselves in a state of weakness and immaturity.

Jesus also promoted the acceptance of contradictions. He made it clear that it is the only way for us to thrive in a hurtful world. Jesus urged for us to be as "shrewd as snakes and harmless as doves" (Matthew 10:16). On the surface this message sounds absurd, but we *can* hold two seemingly different qualities in tension. We don't have to be either humble or self-assertive; we can move between both. We don't have to be either realistic or idealistic; we can have aspects of both. And we don't have to be entirely on the left or right side of any issue; our beliefs can fall across the spectrum of standardized politics. If only our culture could understand this. If only our political parties could respect this. If only we as a population could grow beyond dualistic thinking, perhaps we could enter a world of maturity and growth.

Jesus, himself, *was* the ultimate contradiction. Both God and man, perfect in every way on one side, and prone to humanity's limitations on the other. Yet he held it perfectly in tension. Humans are not simple beings, and our spirituality is anything but simple and resolvable. For many of us there is no other way to find truth in our lives than to accept our contradictions and to accept the tension that we are many different things—strong and weak, loving and hurtful, well-intentioned and selfish, educated and ignorant.

When we do accept these contradictions, we are capable of vast new depths of understanding, and we are capable of much greater expanses of love, peace, and perspective. Perhaps we are even filled with the presence of our Creator when we learn to appreciate our contradictions. Perhaps, like Christ, this is when we can truly live in union with God.

The Means

As you seek truth in your life, it's important to consider how you seek it. The manner in which we seek answers can determine whether or not we end up with good choices. And good choices are simply those that bear good *fruit*—good thoughts, actions, behaviors, and habits. Know also that it can help tremendously to connect with people in your life who exhibit and exemplify goodness. It can clarify your understanding of what is good in every situation. It can also influence you to desire and seek goodness more often. So find people in your life who seek truth in sincere, healthy, and uplifting manners. Their example will lead you to sincere, healthy, and uplifting choices. For what it's worth, one such example can be found in the master of life.

Christians often limit the significance of Jesus to the spiritual realm. They raise images and sculptures of him at the front of churches and then bow down to his spiritual prowess. But there is also profound value in looking at him as a man. He provided an incredible example of how to approach life as a living, breathing human being. It was flawless, and it can be so empowering. I encourage you to read the Gospels, the first four book of the New Testament, and look at how Jesus approached every situation and challenge.

Look at how *thoughtfully* he read, discussed, and related holy texts.

Look at how *confidently* he questioned the expectations of religious authorities.

Look at how *assertively* he confronted small-minded assumptions about religious practices.

Look at how *lovingly* he recognized people who identified their truths.

Look at how *consistently* he demanded awareness of cultural and human shortcomings.

Look at how *sincerely* he spoke to the crowds that followed him.

Look at how *humbly* he interacted with people who were not thinking on his level.

Look at how *fiercely* he valued the present moment, never allowing fear of the future to cripple his efforts.

All these *-ly* words are descriptive attributes. They are adverbs. They describe the *manner* in which Jesus approached life, and they can be so valuable in our searching. They can lift us out of our baggage and smallness when we encounter challenges. They can ground us in sincerity and humility when we face hardships. In his attributes it's almost impossible to find superficiality, self-centeredness, or small-mindedness. The account of his life is devoid of jealousy, resentment, and entitlement—all the things that burden us as we move through life.

Read also what Dr. Martin Luther King, Jr. said about the manner in which we can search for truth: "Let us consider, first, the need for a tough mind, characterized by incisive thinking, realistic appraisal, and decisive judgement. The tough mind is sharp and penetrating, breaking through the crust of legends and myths and sifting the true from the false. The tough-minded individual is astute and discerning. He has a strong, austere quality that makes for firmness of purpose and solidness of commitment. Who doubts that this toughness of mind is one of man's greatest needs?"[7]

Does Dr. King's description of a tough-minded individual seem like a good, effective, and powerful approach to truth? It sure does for me. And it's not about being *tough* in the sense that our culture often describes: obstinate, close-minded, or overpowering. It's about being open, astute, discerning, and willing to see truth in both its ugliest and most beautiful forms. It's about having both the confidence and humility to recognize truth, admit falsities, and acknowledge confusion.

As you search for truth, you may have to look closely at your own life. You may have to stare daringly at yourself in the mirror. This may be the only way to gain an understanding of who you are—your perspective, your habits, your tendencies, and the reasons for them. This can take effort and time. It requires patience and humility. And you might not like everything that you find. But there is so much value in conducting a bold, open-minded, and sincere look at yourself. It might be the only way to find truths inside you.

The Ends

In the introduction of this book, I quoted Tim Keller, a highly respected Christian author and church leader. He said, "Each religion informs its followers that they have 'the truth,' and this naturally leads them to feel superior to those with differing beliefs."[8] Understand that this statement absolutely applies to Christians. We are told that we hold the truth and that it is perfect and absolute. But of course not all aspects of our spiritual and theological understanding are perfectly sound. They can't be. That's because we humans will never fully understand God. We will never fully understand every movement, reasoning, and desire of the Creator of the universe. Nor will we ever fully comprehend every message in the Bible. If we truly believe that the Bible was inspired by God, if we truly believe that the Creator of the universe breathed its Spirit into this book, then we must accept that some of its mysteries and concepts are indeed holy and beyond our grasp. And that's okay. We can keep moving forward in our limited understandings. In fact, that might be the whole point, to continue searching through every phase and circumstance of life and to continue accepting our unknowing.

The Means Are the End

In my life, here is what I know: God is truth. And when I compare Jesus' life and teachings to what is written on my heart, I find absolute truth. His *way* was centered on a life full of love, humility, and selflessness, and there's nothing more truthful than that. But I'm still stuck with the task of living my life and making decisions at every turn. And perhaps that is the answer: his *way*, and the constant pursuit of it, at every step and in every decision.

In John 6:27 Jesus said, "Spend your energy seeking the eternal life that the Son of Man can give you." And in Matthew 7:7–8 he said, "Keep on seeking, and you will find. . . . Everyone who seeks, finds." Pete Rollins offered up the concept that our seeking *is* finding, that the *act* of seeking is actually the answer. As disappointing as this might be, because it doesn't promise perfect resolution, it can relieve the great burden of *expecting* perfect resolution. It can allow us to overcome the temptation to accept simplistic answers that eventually run their course and dissolve into irrelevance. It can help us accept the fact that life never really resolves, that we always live with contradiction and uncertainty, and that the act of seeking good things might be the highest and most noble truth we can ever experience.

PART III: REDISCOVERING

12. QUESTIONS

Questions are so important. Especially in the twenty-first century, an era of rapid technology developments and sweeping culture changes, we must continually search for new answers for our lives. And sometimes, the forming of good questions is just as important as finding answers. I spent four decades in the Christian church and then one day walked away from it without regrets. How did that happen so easily? What was I losing by not attending church? And what was I gaining? To answer these questions, I needed to get away from distractions and spend time listening, and I quickly realized that I wasn't necessarily listening for answers. I was listening for deeper questions. I needed to discover the right questions for my life. I needed to find the most pressing questions, the persistent ones, the ones that were always waiting to be asked after both success and failure, in both prosperity and in hardship.

What matters to me? Who do I want to be? And how do I want to live?

Once these questions were revealed, I found great satisfaction in engaging them. They allowed me to see my life more clearly. They helped me discover why my faith was so important. They helped me determine if my faith was someone else's or if it could serve as my own transforming path toward peace, healing, growth, maturity, and wisdom. And they helped me decide what my life could look like both in prosperity and hardship. That's when these questions became powerful.

Great Questions

I also found that the master of life constantly asked meaningful questions. He must have loved good questions because he asked so many of them, and he almost never answered them for people. Instead he simply seemed to be looking for sincere answers. Here are a few examples of Jesus' questions:

"Why are you afraid?" (Matthew 8:26)
"Who is my mother? And who are my brothers?" (Matthew 12:48)
"Who do you say I am?" (Matthew 16:15)
"Why ask me about what is good?" (Matthew 19:17)
"What do you want me to do for you?" (Matthew 20:32)
"Haven't you ever read the Scriptures?" (Matthew 21:16)
"Why all this commotion and weeping?" (Mark 5:39)
"Can you see anything now?" (Mark 8:23)
"Why do you question this in your hearts?" (Luke 5:22)
"What does the law of Moses say? How do you read it?" (Luke 10:26)
"Why can't you decide for yourselves what is right?" (Luke 12:57)
"Would you like to get well?" (John 5:6)
"Does this offend you?" (John 6:61)
"Do you believe this?" (John 11:26)

These are not leading questions, and they don't have textbook answers. They aren't questions that Jesus asked to see if people could answer them *correctly*. That wouldn't have made them powerful.

Power seemed to lie in his questions when people answered them sincerely. Brian McLaren described Jesus' questioning this way: "In conversation after conversation, Jesus resists being clear or direct. There's hardly ever a question that he simply answers; instead, his answer comes in the form of a question, or it turns into a story, or it is full of metaphors that invite more questions."[1]

In a way, Jesus could be considered a great therapist because he posed questions that encouraged people to work through their confusion. He insisted that they face tough questions and answer them in complete sincerity. Perhaps we should take his love for questions seriously. God knows that our population could use a good therapist.

Go with Questions

When we ask good questions about things that really matter, we can have discussions with almost any person from any part of the world. We can explore good and fruitful living, or our connection with God, or the value of an ancient story with anyone from any culture and any neighborhood. We can do this with someone from India, Japan, Zimbabwe, Peru, Croatia, West Virginia, New Mexico, or Detroit. But so often we just don't. So often we just plant ourselves in the few things that we do know and then focus on our differences, thus, remaining disconnected. And so often we're so concerned with being right that we forget about how important it is to be together. Being together, of course, does not mean that everyone agrees on every topic. That should never be expected, nor is it ever the point. We ask questions together because it brings us together.

Today it appears that people stopped asking questions together. In the church perhaps some people stopped asking questions because they feel satisfied with the answers that people came up with centuries ago. Or they assume that their clergy holds the answers. Others avoid questions entirely because they don't want their traditional answers to be threatened, no matter how sensical or nonsensical they might be.

Rob Bell told a story in a podcast about the frustration that Moses had with the Israelites when they refused to step into the fullness of their spiritual maturity. He pointed out that those ancient people didn't want to stand before God and face their questions. They wanted to stand "at a distance" (Exodus 20:18). They wanted Moses or a newly appointed king to face the hard questions about their faith and their interaction with God. They wanted to avoid these questions and have someone else deliver all the answers.[2] They wanted to remain uninvolved and small. This caused all kinds of tension both in their community and in their faith. I often wonder if church communities today suffer because of the same reasons. Are we afraid to step forward into the mystery of our faith? Are we afraid to face hard questions about our beliefs, our practices, and our lives? Are we afraid to make tough decisions about how to move forward in faith in the twenty-first century?

It can be frightening to face tough questions, and it can be terrifying to face the answers, especially when they compel you to make changes to how you have always done things. But never forget that God gave this gift to you—the gift of choice. And never forget that you are an amazing creation. You have a heart, mind, and spirit that can lead you in your faith journey. You also have an amazing, unfathomable God, capable of peace and presence like you have never known. And you have an amazing example of *life* in Christ. His example is right there for the taking. It's right there in the Gospels. You don't need an authority figure to show you exactly how to follow it. Remember that none of Jesus' disciples possessed degrees from a religious institution. He called guys who fished for a living and collected money for the government. Acts 4:13 says that Peter and John were unschooled, "with no special training in the Scriptures." And those people who did receive formal religious instruction were not always to be trusted. Of all the people Jesus confronted, he seemed to be most critical of the religious leaders. In Mark 12:38 he taught people to "beware of these teachers of religious law!" In Matthew 23 he said seven times, "What sorrow awaits" these teachers and even told a crowd, "don't follow their example" (Matthew 23:3).

John the Baptist likewise blasted religious leaders and called them a "brood of snakes" (Matthew 3:7).

Please understand that this isn't a call to speak out against any religious leader in your life. Rather it's a call for you to step forward and accept your significance in your own spiritual journey. Don't expect someone else to figure it all out for you. You are certainly not the only person wrestling with questions, doubt, and uncertainty. So share this wrestling with others. Articulate your questions to other people, starting with people you trust. And listen to feedback in humility. But don't hide behind the corporate confidence of some institution or tribe. That is the effortless path, and we all know that effortless ventures usually end in satisfaction-less results. Our spirituality doesn't solely exist inside the walls of a church, temple, mosque, or synagogue. If your faith is important, then of course you should have a hand in it!

Share your thoughts on these questions in your homes, at your workplace, at school, at the coffee shop or bar, and certainly in your church. You may be surprised how enthusiastic people are to address new questions that are emerging today. Of course, you might also hit a brick wall of refusal and criticism, but keep focused on your growth, maturity, and wisdom. Reggie McNeal reminds us that churches often have a difficult time accepting this kind of open discussion because there is so much pressure to agree with traditional dogma: "I think a lot of church leaders are intimidated by all the God-interest in the culture at large. I think we don't know how to hold conversations about God. We've only been taught to sell our brand of religion. We are so intent on convincing people that their life is screwed up, their faith is wrong, their beliefs are messed up, and so forth, that we are inept at listening and engaging people. We look at people as 'prospects' for membership rather than spiritual beings with the same quest for God."[3]

Today we don't have to be intimidated. We can be encouraged. The exciting thing is that younger generations might be more ready to work toward stronger spiritual connections than previous generations ever were. That's because so many of them possess the audacity to question God. Dave Kinnaman and Gabe Lyons studied the younger generations and had this to say: "[Younger generations] are the ultimate 'conversation generations.' They want to discuss, debate, and question everything. Young outsiders want to have discussions, but they perceive Christians as unwilling to engage in genuine dialogue. They think of conversations as 'persuasion' sessions, in which the 'Christian' downloads as many arguments as possible."[4]

Maybe the younger generations are in a better position than previous generations ever were to grow a relevant and meaningful faith because they are afraid neither to question it nor discover it. And maybe older generations, who deeply value their loyalty to traditional assumptions and expectations, could take inspiration from young people who are ready to move forward into something deeper, more beautiful, and more profound.

No matter how you approached your faith in the past, don't shy away from your questions. Stare daringly at them. Sit with them so you can begin to answer them. And never be afraid to answer them with sincerity. This is what the man at the center of the Christian religion asked of people two thousand years ago. Maybe his fierce love for sincerity can be the model for your faith in the twenty-first century.

13. HUMILITY

I served under many different types of leaders in the military. The ones who stood out the most were confident, extroverted, and highly vocal. These were the people who quickly got my attention when they walked into a room. I also served under quieter, less vocal leaders. Both types were effective, and these differences were mostly stylistic, not a final determinant in any one person's ability to lead and supervise humans.

The most influential leaders, however—the ones who motivated me both to succeed in my work and to strive to be a better officer, coworker, and person—were the ones who had a special trait. They possessed a trait that was undeniably contagious and impacted the culture of their organization. That trait was humility. These leaders were able not only to get people's attention but also to get people to look critically at themselves, to seek constant improvement, and to identify and manifest value in other people. This kind of leader seemed to be the most effective at not only accomplishing goals but building teams, and individuals. Individuals and their organizations thrived when their leader exhibited humility.

Our Culture

Our culture is constantly promoting self-centeredness, self-promotion, self-defensiveness, and self-pleasure. Sometimes it's hard even to remember that we can serve anything other than ourselves. For most of us, a self-centered approach to life is just habit at this point.

What we often ignore, however, is the short-lived nature of most self-pleasing products and activities. Their benefits wither away fast. Think about anything that we consume: food, drink, clothes, electronics, social media, entertainment. Does the consumption of any of these provide you a strong reason to get out of bed every morning and labor through your day? Think also about our career intentions: increased salaries, promotions, commissions, investments, retirement plans, and pensions. Do any of these provide you a profound reason to be alive? What would happen if they were suddenly diminished or taken away? Would a stock market crash or sudden unemployment be a reason to call it quits? As necessary as career and financial pursuits are, as much as we are in the habit of putting them first in our lives, they are by themselves a poor foundation for lasting meaning and fulfillment.

We may be innately aware of this, but habits are hard to break. Today we are accustomed to serving ourselves. This is no surprise. We want to be served, and we want to be served promptly. That's fine. That's our reality. But have you ever felt like there is more out there? Have you ever felt like there is a better way to live? Have you ever felt like you are missing out on something bigger? And have you ever felt like you totally could find something deeper and better and bigger, but you're just stuck in an endless circle of self-importance? I have, and I often feel lost in that space. That space can produce a profound emptiness for me.

The Most Powerful Human Trait

It seems like an expectation in our culture to constantly put our importance on display. We expend great efforts to portray ourselves as strong, beautiful, and successful. These words are important to us. We often associate importance with people who possess these attributes. Strength is such a highly valued trait today. Outward beauty is rewarded with attention. Financial or career success is often a means toward receiving respect. But I often wonder, would someone who truly is important ever need to display that they are? Wouldn't the reality of it prove itself? If someone really was strong, beautiful, and successful, wouldn't they know it? And if they really knew it, would they still feel a need to display it?

The most impressive people, the most influential people, the most admirable people are often the ones who put no emphasis on their importance. They make no effort to portray themselves as strong, beautiful, or successful. When we see them, they just *are* those things, without hesitation or explanation. They enter a situation, and they are influential. They face a formidable challenge, and they are strong. They can stand beside anyone and be beautiful. They embark on a project, and they are successful, in some worthy manner.

Of course, no one is strong, beautiful, and successful in every circumstance. All humans find themselves in awkward, unbecoming situations. Even the people we admire most are not comic book superheroes with endless resources of confidence and strength. They are humans, just like us. They experience moments of insignificance, failure, and weakness, just like the rest of us. And just like us they feel unimportant, weak, ugly, and unsuccessful at times. Some of us feel that way quite often. But no matter how we feel about our present circumstances, we can still have influence. We can still exhibit beauty, and we can still show our strength. We can do this without changing any part of ourselves, or attaining any amount of wealth, or achieving any degree of social status. We only have to invite one trait into the flow of our lives. That trait is humility, and it is so very much worth pursuing. Consider the qualities of humility:

Humility is not achieved. To experience it, we simply invite it.
Humility gets us no credit. Rather it gives credit to others.
Humility helps us gain nothing in terms of wealth or assets. It
rewards only our hearts.
Humility is never the first to speak. It always listens.
Humility is never the first to take. It always gives.
Humility does not need to justify. It speaks with pure confidence.
Humility does not show pride. It only shows respect.
Humility does not need to overtake. It is always willing to step
back.
Humility does not look to dominate. It looks to uplift.
Humility does not need to be right. It only seeks truth.
Humility may not always get noticed, but it is stunningly beautiful.

Are you catching on to the attractive and influential qualities of this massively undervalued human trait? Are you comprehending the positive impact it can have on the world? And do you see how our shallow, small-minded culture is so blind to it, and confuses it with weakness? Humility might actually be the purest form of strength, because it is the kind of strength that does not need to be strong. It is the kind of influence that does not need to be influential. It is the kind of beauty that does not need to be noticed.

Whether we experience incredible success or embarrassing failure in our careers, we can still invite humility to govern our perspectives. Whether our relationships are full of generosity and connection or resentment and separation, we can still invite humility to influence our interactions. Whether someone shows us great respect or a lack of courtesy, humility can guide us toward more beautiful responses. Humility has a profound influence on the human heart when it is on display. Its ultimate purpose is to respect, uplift, and give strength to others. And in the process, it shows incredible beauty in the person exhibiting it. And best of all, humility only produces good fruit in our lives (Matthew 7:17).

Do you want to spend your life *portraying* yourself as important, or do you actually want to *be* influential? Do you want to *look* like you are doing great things, or do you actually want to *produce* good things in your life? Of course, we want the latter. We want to *experience* good things, not just talk about them.

A Revolution

Humility can be revolutionary for anyone who invites it into his or her life, and there was a guy who lived two thousand years ago who showed us the perfect example of it. It's no coincidence that he became the most influential man in all of history. Consider the following stories about Jesus' example of humility from the Gospels.

John 2 — Water into Wine

Jesus and his entourage were invited to a wedding party, but the host ran out of wine. So he quietly turned six jars of water into premium wine. And there is no evidence that Jesus took any credit. There is no mention of his desire for people to know that God did something miraculous. Nor is there any request for adoration or worship. Perhaps Jesus simply wanted to uplift the people at the wedding so they could have a better party.

John 4 — The Woman at the Well

Jesus ignored his culture's expectations to hate, vilify, and marginalize this woman even though he had every reason to do so. In his culture, people considered his race and religion to be better than hers. He had status. He had privilege. He knew it, yet he gave it no credence. He ducked below his status and privilege to connect with this woman, to uplift her.

Mark 4 — Calming the Seas

Jesus was sleeping on a boat during a storm. The guys in the boat were frightened. Jesus woke up. He yelled at the weather and everything turned calm. Then he confronted their smallness. He made no mention of his astounding act. He demanded no adoration, worship, or even gratitude. There was no mention of his power, only his desire for those guys to step up and have a more expansive faith.

Matthew 9, Mark 2, and Luke 15 — Hookers, Thieves, and Disreputable Sinners

Jesus didn't need to hang out with people who affirmed his greatness or elevated his social status. He hung out with regular people who had poor reputations: prostitutes, tax collectors, and other "disreputable sinners" (Matthew 9:10). He sat down with them for meals. He went to their homes. He spent quality time with them. He didn't make them change their ways or rise to his holy stature first. He just connected with them, inspired them, helped them, and healed them.

Matthew 18 — The Greatest

Jesus said, "Anyone who becomes as humble as this little child is the greatest in the Kingdom of heaven" (Matthew 18:4). He said that humility can make *anyone* great. Greatness, in this case, is not concerned with physical strength, outward beauty, or financial success. It's about lowering oneself and lifting others up.

How We Become Humble

Humility is a central theme in Jesus' Sermon on the Mount, and there is an undeniable correlation between it and the experience of deep blessings. The beatitudes in Matthew 5 don't describe people who are in a good place. They don't describe people living in comfort or privilege. They don't describe people who are experiencing professional, social, and financial success. Instead, they describe people who are in downright awful situations. Jesus referred to "those who are poor," "those who mourn," "those who hunger and thirst for justice," and "those who are persecuted for doing right" (Matthew 5:3–10). And when we are in these situations, isn't that when our arrogant pride is absent? Whether we choose to release it or it's ripped from us, aren't these situations when pride departs? And isn't this when humility enters? It is for me. And according to the man at the center of the Christian religion, this is when we are truly blessed.

For many of us today, this concept conflicts with what we often assume, that we are blessed when earthly success finds us. Our culture tells us this at every turn, that life gets really good when we experience professional, social, and financial success. We see this everywhere, and so often we buy into it. But Jesus actually said it's the opposite. Could that be because when we are down, that's when we are the most grounded? Could it be when we are stuck in awful situations, our arrogant pride is often replaced by humility? Is that when our hearts are purified—through trial, hardship, pain, and conflict? Could that be when we truly experience peace? And could that be when we truly experience God and the life that Jesus spoke of?

The onset of humility may be one of the keys to experiencing the eternal life that Jesus spoke of. And perhaps this is a new way to look at trials, hardship, pain, and conflict—that these unwanted moments are where we experience true living! That's because these moments often result in the release of a great burden—the burden of carrying our pride and self-importance. This is when our spirits are free. This is how we receive great blessings, as Jesus described in the Sermon on the Mount. And maybe this is when we are most alive! This perspective on hardship can provide a purer, healthier way to look at both failure and success. Perhaps we can finally understand that professional, social, and financial success—as helpful as it is for our families and our livelihoods—often prevents us from truly living.

Humility could be an incredible option for our lives in the twenty-first century. It could invite so much beauty into our lives. It can strengthen our relationships. It can uplift our organizations and communities. It can actually change the world around us. But we must understand that our culture rarely speaks of it. That's because our culture has a hard time recognizing it. Humility is often misidentified as weakness. Our culture is obsessed with self-importance and self-centeredness, so understand that when you commit to the trait of humility, you will rarely be commended. You might not be noticed. Instead, you might be criticized by our shallow, self-serving culture. But know that humility touches people deeply. Trust that it will do that! And if you need an example, look to the man at the center of the Christian religion. Read about him. See how his actions and words were grounded in humility, even though he clearly had the ability to rise above, overtake, and dominate people. This man, Jesus, was the embodiment of humility, and he ended up being perhaps the most influential man in history.

14. MATURITY

One of my favorite people to discuss the Bible with is an atheist friend. We have great conversations about the Bible, how it was written, and how people interpret it. I enjoy talking with him about the Bible because he's actually interested in what it says. He even read through its entirety recently. The reasoning he gave for reading such a very long book that means so very little to him: "I want to know what I'm talking about." He wanted to have some amount of knowledge and understanding when discussing the Bible with his Christian friends. I so appreciated that statement because it was mature. He didn't want to enter a discussion about people's faith in an ignorant manner. Nor did he want to write off people who believe something different than he does. He wanted to see their side of the discussion. It showed that he was open-minded, willing to learn, and even willing to have his mind changed.

I wish more Christians would do the same. I wish it was more common for Christians to read the Bible with care and an understanding of how it was written. This is not because I hope for all people everywhere to come to the same conclusions as mine. Rather it's so they can better understand *why* they believe the things they do. Those of us who grew up in the Christian faith were taught what the

Bible says, its stories and most notable verses. We also were told what
the Bible "says"—in other words, how it is to be interpreted and what
conclusions are to be made. This is what Christian schools, seminar-
ies, churches, and weekly sermons teach—the "right" way to believe
and understand the Christian faith. But what's often left out of that
process is an appreciation for people's freedom to discover their own
understandings. Often times in church communities, young people
are taught a system of belief and practice, but then they are never
encouraged to question it and determine throughout their lives if that
system still works.

For example, I used to read the story of Noah's ark in Genesis like
it actually happened. It was only a few years ago that I discovered the
value of *not* reading that story literally, and this is what actually
brought me more passionately back into the practice of Bible reading.
It brought the Old Testament forward into my life.

As a kid I was taught that the story of Noah's ark was real, and
that's what made it powerful. I was in awe of the depiction of two of
every animal species walking in an orderly fashion onto a big boat. To
my six-year-old self, that was an important way to learn who God is:
awesome, powerful, and present. A literal reading is a great way to
teach the story of Noah's ark to a little kid. But as an adult I learned
that the account of Noah and the flood was likely a retelling of a
much older Babylonian (pagan) cultural myth. As an adult then, the
story of Noah's ark wasn't just about oohing and aahing at every
amazing miracle. Nor was it about the fear of God's wrath. It's a story
about me. It's about my faith in the midst of harsh and uncertain
times. It's about doing what's right even when I get mocked. And that
makes it meaningful. That's even what makes it truth-filled for me,
regardless of the amount of factual data in the story. The story of
Noah's ark didn't prove anything to me as much as it offered me
lessons about my life, my faith, and my choices.

Other parts of the Bible are written like they are historical
accounts. Much of the four Gospels and the book of Acts, for example, seem to be written largely as dispassionate recordings of events.
So that's a good way to read them, even though we still find inconsis-

tencies and disagreements between them. But if many of those Old Testament stories are to be relevant in my life, I must move beyond the assumption that they prove anything about the events of the past and instead allow them to teach me profound and meaningful lessons for my life today.

Mature Faith

There is an unfortunate tradition in Christianity to approach complex topics in manners that are less than mature, and it's difficult to confront. I believe that a mature perspective, one that is rooted in our 21st-century realities, is an effective way to engage our faith today and move it into our lives. It could also heal many of the deep wounds caused and perpetuated by institutional religion. This chapter will not pass without criticism. It could stir up debate. It could even be seen as controversial. That's fine. In fact, that might be a good thing. What better way to honor and worship our Creator than to approach our faith and the Bible with an open heart, mind, and spirit—or as Jesus said in John 4:23, "in spirit and in truth."

Some people will feel their faith being threatened in this chapter. If that's true for you, then I urge you to take account of your faith. Consider how it came to you. Look clearly at your assumptions, your foundations, and your responses when something threatens them. Find out what areas of your faith are mature and what areas easily crack and crumble.

A mature Christian faith will not get defensive at the first hint that our Bibles might not be a completely factual document. Perhaps when we get angry over a concept that threatens part of our belief system, that belief system might actually be quite fragile and built upon shaky ground. In Luke 6:48 Jesus made it clear that our faith should be built on a solid foundation: "It is like a person building a house who digs deep and lays the foundation on solid rock. When the floodwaters rise and break against that house, it stands firm because it is well built." And Jesus' teachings were filled with encouragement for people to build their faith with clarity and maturity.

Unfortunately, many Christians have not been taught how to build a mature faith. A mature faith works through the challenges, questions, and criticisms that it encounters. This is how our faith grows, but this can also cause it to change, and sometimes it can cause it to crumble. And when that happens, we have an opportunity to build a new foundation, one that is ours, and that's when it can be powerful and relevant in our lives.

Mature Growth

Maturity is required for true spiritual awareness and growth. Maturity, in this context, implies the distancing of ourselves from childish ways. Children must learn as children do. They learn best when they engage concepts and definitions that are appropriate for their mental and emotional stages. The same should be true for adults, but so often we have worked with concepts surrounding our faith that are appropriate for children. This could be a big reason why so many adults no longer look to the church to manage their faith. Perhaps they don't care to engage a childish version of it.

We would never ask a college physics major to take a second grade math quiz. And we would never ask a professional athlete to follow a middle school exercise regimen. That would be inappropriate. It wouldn't be helpful. Neither should adults build their faith on childish frameworks. Hopefully all of us approach our faith and our Creator with the humility of a child like Jesus said in Matthew 18 and 19. But when he said to "become like little children," he wasn't telling us to become gullible or just to believe any and every idea that's placed in front of us (Matthew 18:3). Perhaps he was talking about an openness and willingness to learn, discover, and grow. Because he also told us to "look beneath the surface" in John 7:24. And perhaps we should take seriously what Paul articulated in 1 Corinthians 13:11 when he said, "When I was a child, I spoke and thought and reasoned as a child. But when I grew up, I put away childish things."

As children we were not mature. Our minds were simple, limited, and willing to accept almost anything that a figure of authority presented. We were introduced to the faith of our parents, teachers, and pastors. But because this faith was not ours, as we grew into adulthood, many of us naturally stopped connecting with it. A step was missing for many of us. We weren't encouraged to question it, and we therefore stopped growing with it.

Religious curriculum can be a wonderful system to raise children in loving, structured, spiritual, and civic-minded frameworks. But as we age, there comes a point where we detach from childish systems. Our developing independence breaks us from them so we can then grow as adults. Naturally, we begin to question what we were taught. Hopefully all religious curriculum eventually includes some analysis and criticism of its beliefs. Unfortunately, we rarely see this in practice. And for many people the absence of criticism equates religious instruction to brainwashing—the promotion of blind acceptance of other people's interpretations of an ancient book. Kids will believe almost anything we tell them. The same is not true for adults. Adults can question and critique. And as we have seen across our society, adults will reject religious curriculum when it no longer works in their lives.

If this doesn't sit well with you, look at the number of people who were raised in Catholic schools but no longer practice the Catholic faith as adults. Look at how many people were raised in Lutheran, Presbyterian, and Baptist churches but no longer attend them as adults. In my life I couldn't count the number of acquaintances who grew up in the church but stopped attending as adults. If you don't know many people like this in your life, look at the statistics. The Pew Research Center and the Public Religion Research Institution laid it out for us. Being raised and instructed in Christian communities does not equate to participation in them as adults.[1]

The need for more mature systems of spiritual growth in church communities is undeniable. Father Richard Rohr said, "Most churches just keep doing the first half of life over and over again. Young people are made to think that . . . believing a few doctrines or performing some rituals is all religion is about. The would-be maturing believer is not challenged to adult faith or service to the world."[2] Without an appreciation for our maturing beliefs about God, faith, and spirituality; without an understanding that we will, at some point, toss aside childish assumptions; the foundations of our religious training, those beliefs and assumptions that were handed to us, can simply become trivia. And eventually they could become trivial, like they are today for millions of people. Today many of us are underserved by institutional Christianity. We need more, and we need something mature.

Maturity and the Bible

The Christian faith gives centrality to the Bible. The Bible is an ancient book, and it sure would make sense to approach it as such. It was written by ancient people, for ancient people. It is filled with scholarly techniques and tendencies that were unique to ancient writings. The Bible is not a history book like the ones we read today. Modern Western authors of history value facts and evidence. Ancient writers did not. Ancient writers were often superstitious, much more than we are today, and they passed down their histories verbally, over the course of generations. Historical accuracy was not always the primary intent. Ancient writers also embraced myth and wonder. They embraced mysticism in their histories. These concepts and their assumptions are woven throughout the stories and accounts that we find in the Bible, particularly in the Old Testament.

Ancient writers often interpreted historic events according to what they assumed were the desires of God, or the gods. We see this in everything from ancient Egyptian hieroglyphs to ancient Jewish texts to Homer's *The Iliad* and *The Odyssey*. In these ancient texts, God or the gods may not have actually *willed* every event in their history, but that's often how ancient people accounted for them. Ancient humans documented historical developments in good faith, but this documentation was not separated from their view of the world. And biblical writers wrote their books through the eyes of their faith, but also with superstition, wonder, and mysticism. God's divine inspiration may have been present when these ancient authors sat down to write, but that doesn't mean that every word they penned was based in perfect historical accuracy. God may not have actually said many of the words documented by the authors of the Old Testament. God may not have actually caused every Old Testament battle or event to turn out the way it did. God's interaction with the ancient Israelites might have actually been far less obvious and deliberate than we read in the Bible. Or maybe it was exactly like it was described. We can never know. We do know, however, that those ancient authors wrote about God's work according to their perceptions, and that involved significant amounts of superstition, wonder, and mysticism.

This is not a refute of any *truth* in the Bible. In fact, it brings the *truths* of these ancient stories to life! But perhaps it's a different kind of truth. Perhaps now the truths we discover as we read the stories of Noah, Moses, King David, or Jeremiah are found in the concepts they reveal in our lives, not simply the truth of whether those ancient events occurred. Perhaps we can learn a lot about ourselves, our world, and how we interact with God when we read these old stories.

Consider what Bible scholar and author Peter Enns notices in Genesis 6:7 where God decides to "destroy every living thing" on the planet. Enns shows that God "finds things out" about humans; God "regrets and laments" creation; God was "caught off-guard" by it.[3] This description of God is inconsistent with so much of the rest of the Bible, where God is described as omnipotent and omniscient. Enns reveals that these verses in Genesis describe a God that appears to be small-minded, with all kinds of limitations, imperfections, and shortcomings, sort of like a human. Isn't that interesting? It sounds like the author of Genesis didn't actually possess perfect knowledge of God's qualities. It sounds like the author wondered and made assumptions about God's involvement in the world. It sounds like the author was searching for reasons why God did such awful things to people. And isn't that exactly what we do today?

What about all the descriptions of God as jealous and vengeful? In Ezekiel 39 God laid out a detailed plan to wipe out the lesser god Gog and all its followers. God threatened to bring this pagan god down, drag him along, and send fire down on people who followed him because he would not allow his holy name to be profaned. Is this really a sensible description of our unfathomable God? Other parts of the Bible describe God's nature as loving, forgiving, and full of gentleness and self-control (Galatians 5:22–23). This description in Ezekiel makes God sound like an angry Army general who was embarrassed on the battlefield, jealous and vengeful. Is our Creator prone to bouts of anger and violence, like so many humans when things don't go their way? Does God really sit and stew or throw temper tantrums, like we do when someone pisses us off? And does God really get so angry at humans that he sometimes suddenly needs to kill a bunch of us? Does this sound like God, or does it sound like some of history's rulers who brought terror and anguish into the world while fully believing that God supported their efforts?

Humans, even the God-fearing ones, are notorious for personifying God in their own image. As the great philosopher Voltaire once said, "In the beginning God created man in his own image, and man has been trying to return the favor ever since." It appears that Old Testament authors sometimes interpreted events according to their limited assumptions about God. Sometimes they described God as grand and expansive, and sometimes God was small, petty, jealous, and obsessed with revenge. They used all kinds of contradictory descriptions of God because they were figuring out what life's events and experiences meant. They were trying to understand how God worked in their lives and what God communicated to them. And that is awesome. Because that's exactly what we do today! Those Old Testament authors struggled with the same questions we do! What is God? What does God want? What is God doing? What does any of this mean?! They made assumptions like we do when they answered those questions. So now we can open our Bibles and read about circumstances, challenges, and choices that mirror our own. We can read about stories that provide insight into a life of faith. The actual historical events may not have unfolded exactly the way they are depicted, but they can still offer profound lessons. They may not always provide any sort of clear answer for us, but they can clarify exactly what we are facing today: choices, specifically in determining how we should live and move in communion with our Creator.

This Bible of ours is so much richer and offers so much more than what we are often taught. It offers so much more depth and expansiveness than what we often give it credit for. If we gain an appreciation for circumstances, challenges, and choices that all humans face, then the Bible can help us gain profound insight into our lives today. It can help us see our lives better. It may not always provide clear and perfect solutions, but it may eventually guide us to greater wisdom. And isn't that the experience of God: gleaning wisdom to help us make beautiful, impactful, and profound choices, rather than just obeying orders? Reggie McNeal made this point: "In the last gasps of the modern church, we have made Bible study in itself a mark of spiritual maturity, clearly missing the major evidence of what God looks for in his search for spiritual maturity—our relationship to him and to people. The Pharisees studied the Scripture and knew it better than any other group, but Jesus chided them for missing the point."[4]

Many people want clear guidance. They want a person, a book, or a god to tell them what to do. Of course, we all want this sometimes. It's hard work to make decisions, and sometimes we need help in making them. We look to God, to mentors, and to peers to help us. But it's also part of our nature to sometimes avoid tough decisions, just like it's in our nature to sometimes avoid blame for our actions and decisions. If we can claim that we followed someone else's authoritative instruction, then we really can't be blamed for the consequences. Instead, we can claim innocence due to our uninvolvement, like a robot that had its behavior programmed. And this is the definition of an immature life. An immature life shies away from the hard work of choice and therefore has a hard time accepting consequences. So when we read our Bibles, perhaps what we should seek is not answers, but wisdom, so we can make good choices.

Maturity and Language

Another area where we might question our maturity is in our communication with each other. The church speaks a particular language, and if it wants to start a discussion with more people—at least more people than just the ones sitting in its pews—it must accept both where its language adds value and where it hinders communication. This could be an awkward shift for many Christians, but it might be an effective way to communicate outside church buildings.

Christians love to refer to Jesus as *King* and Christendom as God's *kingdom*. It's prevalent throughout prayers, liturgy, and music. But who else uses these words today? Two thousand years ago the metaphor of Jesus as a king was an effective tool to explain the potential influence he could have in people's lives—no one greater to look up to. The ancient world was dominated by kings. So was Europe hundreds of years later when biblical texts were translated into the English language. It was, in fact, an English king in the 1600s who ordered a translation of the Bible into what would famously be called the King James Version. There was no higher authoritative reference than a king at that time. But for many people today it's a strange concept to refer to Jesus or God as a king. It's awkward to refer to any part of the world as a kingdom. It's not helpful to picture Jesus on a throne next to his Father, who sits on an even bigger throne (Hebrews 12:2). It's abnormal to use phrases like "crowns of righteousness" (2 Timothy 4:8) and "scepter of justice" (Hebrews 1:8). This imagery relates to no part of our lives today.

Worship the *King*. He sits at the *right hand* of God. He sits on a *throne*. The *kingdom* will have no end because he *reigns* forever. These words are ancient. Their significance is ancient. Of course, Christians will continue to use these words within their organizations, but no one speaks like that today outside church buildings. Many people have never thought of Jesus' influence in their lives in the context of a royal court, nor do they need to. From what we know, Jesus possessed very little resemblance to the demeanor of earthly royalty, and his behavior hardly resembled the manner in which kings and queens have conducted themselves over the course of history. Especially in America, where we take great pride in snubbing kings and seceding from their kingdoms, these words sound antiquated and foreign. Perhaps that's why they lack significance outside the church.

Paul may have sometimes referred to Jesus as Lord simply because it referenced Caesar's power and influence. In Greek, the "pledge of allegiance" in the Roman Empire was *Caesar ho Kurios*— Caesar is Lord.[5] That phrase was established before anyone knew Jesus. So when Paul stated that "Jesus Christ is Lord" in Philippians 2:11, it made great sense for his audience because it signified the profound influence that Jesus could have in their lives. It was highly relevant language for them. People understood that it was a life-altering choice to submit to Jesus and not just Caesar. And it wasn't just a statement about Christ's grand spiritual status. It was a statement that when people allowed Jesus to have influence in their lives, they also gave Caesar diminishing influence. This was a bold and risky thing to say two thousand years ago in the Mediterranean world. Today, however, the meaning can get lost.

Like Paul did two thousand years ago, we need to communicate the power of God in a language that matters today. We want language that connects us to each other. We want language to have meaning. We want to feel it. And if we want to communicate with people about how incredibly influential Jesus is in our lives, we must learn how to articulate it. And for many people today, kings and kingdoms don't cut it. Thrones and scepters just don't work. Not like they once did. Paul even spelled it out for us in 1 Corinthians 14:9: "If you speak to people in words they don't understand, how will they know what you are saying? You might as well be talking into empty space."

This is not a rejection of the Bible. Our Bibles possess language that was profound for many cultures, but we are in a new era. Nor is this an issue of how we address God. God will abide no matter what language we speak or what names we use. The problem is how we communicate with each other. How can we communicate with our friends, neighbors, and coworkers if we are stuck in language that they don't use? No one is proposing that we call Jesus the President of our hearts, the Founder of our lives, or the CEO of our souls. Certainly those metaphors lack in profundity. But this point about language exposes how poorly Christian institutions communicate outside their congregations in the twenty-first century. Perhaps this is a significant reason why millions of people, especially the younger generations, are no longer in communication with the church.

One interesting example of language that communicates something profound about our faith today is in Kent R. Hunter's book *Restoring Civility*. He described the concept of the kingdom of God as *culture*—how we think and act. This word is absolutely relevant today. We know what it means, how it affects our lives, and how it reflects upon us. We use it in business, education, politics, entertainment, and many other areas of our society. I've heard the phrase *the kingdom of God* used in hundreds of sermons, and the most common definitions that preachers have assigned to it vary from land features to political borders to church communities and even a sort of spiritual "cloud" that floats through parts of the earth. Each definition was useful in the context of its discussion, but *culture* . . . this word is relevant in many contexts today. It directly applies to many parts of our lives. Hunter talked about the impact that Jesus' words and actions had on people. He said that Jesus "focused on culture. . . . He infused it into his followers. He modeled it." And "it was infectious."[6] A discussion about having a *culture* that resembles Jesus' *way* can be profound today. It moves the discussion into our homes, neighborhoods, workplaces, and social media interactions.

At some point, if we are to share with others what moves us deeply, we need to learn how to communicate it effectively. We must learn to articulate the power of our faith experience in 21st-century language, or it won't be received. It won't connect, and it won't work. Like Jesus said, "No one puts new wine into old wineskins" (Mark 2:22).

Think about words that you use in describing something that is meaningful to you. Think about what God means to you. Think about how this faith can be alive in every moment of your life. Think about how you can describe these things. This is not about rejecting spiritual or biblical concepts; it is about recognizing them in the context of our lives. It is about naming them. It is about acknowledging them in the fullness of our maturity.

Maturity in the Elephant's Room

In the same way that every culture develops its own means of effective communication, its perspectives on morality also change and develop over time. Eugene Peterson, the great modern-day translator of the Bible, put it this way: "Every generation faces a changed culture, different social problems and challenges, new patterns of work, evolving economic and political conditions. Much of what a Christian community in each generation does is learn together how this is done in its particular circumstances."[7]

Not all Christians believe that a man should be killed if he commits murder. This is capital punishment, and consensus will never be reached on that issue among practicing Christians. Yet that is what God explicitly told humans to do in Genesis 9. Divorce and remarriage are commonly accepted in our culture, yet Jesus and Paul spoke against it (Mark 10 and 1 Corinthians 7:10–11). The books of Leviticus and Deuteronomy are filled with strict religious and cultural rules, but hardly any of them are followed today. Social values, expectations, and laws change over time. They are unique to different cultures. They change as cultures change. This is true for all of history. But the Christian religion is notorious for denying this reality.

The denial of social and cultural development could be another reason why so many people are turned off by the church. Many churches adhere to doctrine that was established hundreds of years ago by white, European men. It's interesting how much our culture has changed since Renaissance and medieval times yet so many Christians still assume that the opinions of these dead men should guide us. The church's reluctance over interpretational revisions is startling. We even see how stubbornly the church denies that its own leaders have changed their opinion on what God's Word *says* throughout history. This is one reason why we have so many distinct Christian denominations today. They all developed through different "cultural lenses or postures," as Bible scholar Wil Gafney has pointed out.[8]

Moral relativism is present throughout the Bible. It's present through history. It's present throughout the Christian religion. It has always been present, and it always will be as long as humans are practicing it. Moral relativism is about choice, something that every person in every culture faces. It's about exercising our God-given freedoms, understanding the era in which we live, and deciding where our values lie. It is a gift that we should embrace. Yet so many Christians curse the very thought of moral relativism and accuse people of heresy when it is exhibited. Perhaps this is why so many people today can't take the church seriously. Why would they, when the church doesn't take awareness of itself seriously?

Maturity over Ancient Customs

If you are having a hard time with the concept of moral relativism and its existence throughout Christian culture, look at how morality, spiritual practice, and views on social justice changed from ancient times to today. Start with Bilhah and Zilpah. Look up their story in Genesis 30. Consider their side of it. By our standards today, these women were sexually abused by a God-fearing man. Think for a second about how Jacob, a celebrated titan of the Old Testament, would spend time in prison today for his behavior.

Look up all the women David had affairs with in First and Second Samuel. Forget Bathsheba. Look at all the other women with which he had adulterous flings, at least by our standards. David had many wives and concubines by virtue of his kingship. Today we would label him an adulterer and a serial bigamist.

Slavery was even upheld as a common and morally acceptable practice both by humans and God in the Bible. Reverend Wil Gafney pointed out that it was normalized in the Bible. She said that in many instances "the text endorses slavery and sometimes God endorses slavery."[9] It's alarming when Christians declare that everything in the Bible should be accepted at face value as truth for our lives. Perhaps these declarations help explain why slavery continued for centuries without effective opposition. Perhaps today we should especially celebrate the people who sought a new morality in regard to issues of slavery. Those folks actually had to refute the Bible!

Look also at how morality, spiritual practice, and views on social justice changed within the timeline of the Bible. Throughout the Old Testament, violence and revenge were affirmed by God. Exodus 21 contains laws that promoted violent payback with the concept of "an eye for an eye." But as Dr. Miguel A. De La Torre, a religion professor and author, points out, Jesus completely rejected it in Matthew 5:39. Jesus said to deny the notion of violent payback and "offer the other cheek."[10] Jesus promoted a more generous and nonviolent reaction to offenses than ancient Jewish Law demanded. He was telling people to change their opinions on their holy text.

Joshua, a great Israelite leader, told his army to commit genocide as "an offering to the Lord" in Joshua 6:17. And in 1 Samuel 15, God apparently told Israelite leaders to kill "men, women, children, babies," etc. because he wanted to "settle accounts" with the Amalekites. But in Matthew 6:14, as De La Torre emphasized, Jesus spoke against these behaviors by promoting love and forgiveness in our response to wrongdoing.[11]

The point here is not to prove that the Bible has moral and instructional inconsistencies. Anyone who has the slightest working knowledge of the Bible knows that to be the case. The point is to expose Christianity's acceptance of moral relativism. It's the elephant in the room, and it's time we simply recognize it because anyone who has eyes to see (Ezekiel 12:2) can spot this large and undeniable truth within Christian culture. When we view our faith with maturity and we get past the taboo nature of moral relativism, then we can accept that it is neither sinful nor heretical. As Jesus proved, it's a reality for every generation of Christians, and there's no way to escape it.

Maturity and Sexual Orientation

Homosexuality is always a hot topic in Christianity, and in the twenty-first century we should not avoid it. But if we are to consider it, we should do so with maturity. We must understand that some people can read a few verses in Scripture and contend that they condemn a lifestyle, even one that is defined by beauty, love, and sincerity. But that's just one way to interpret those verses. And as we understand today, there are other many ways to interpret them. Leaders in the Christian faith may call homosexuals sinful, but God certainly may not. And today millions of Christ followers might not either.

There are only a handful of verses in the Bible that directly address homosexuality. Half are in the Old Testament and half are in the New Testament. Homosexual acts within certain contexts are condemned in these verses, but they are not condemned in all contexts. And condemnation of a homosexual life is absent from the Bible. Jesus never condemned it. Statements that Jesus made about relationships, divorce, and adultery are sometimes assumed to apply to sexual orientation, but that's a small-minded way to approach them (Matthew 19). In his teachings about relationships Jesus was far more focused on the promotion of love and its fruit (Matthew 7:17). In Matthew 19 he spoke about men and women becoming one, but the lesson we can take away is not focused on the sexual organs of the partners; it's about becoming one in profoundly deeper ways than just physical interaction. It's about love and a deep union. In Mark 10 he talks about men and women joining together and not separating. This was a response to a question about divorce. So the point is not about male and female body parts; it's about relationships, being joined together and remaining together in love, rather than being separated by adultery, which he addresses in verses 11 and 12. These are big, important topics for all humans to consider. And today's culture is crying out for a mature lesson on love and relationships. Unfortunately, we often get bogged down in petty semantics about who is allowed to be attracted to whom, and who is allowed to express love to whom, and what sexual organs are allowed to touch each other. Regardless of how Christians have approached this topic in the past, today we can think bigger, and we can allow the fullness of our maturity to guide us.

Jesus never addressed the ambiguities of sexual orientation. It sure would be great if he cleared it up for his followers, but he didn't. One reason is perhaps because these topics were not addressed in his culture. They have been largely avoided by most cultures throughout history, and isn't that disconcerting? It reveals how easily humans avoid mature discussions. Some Christians assume that Jesus' statements covered every aspect of the topic of sexual orientation, and they have every right to remain in their beliefs. It's their choice to read his words that way. But for so many of us today, we are ready to read these verses with a new heart, a bigger heart, one that embraces the expansive love of Christ and all of our awe and wonder about God's creation. Pope Francis said this about all matters of faith: "Think big! Open your heart!"[12] That approach makes perfect sense for this topic. So let's do just that: talk about homosexuality with maturity, and a big and open heart.

The Old Testament is filled with rules for living, many of which hold little relevance for us today. The book of Leviticus is filled with rules on morality, all of which were apparently either proclaimed by God or God-fearing leaders. But does any sect of Christianity follow them entirely? Does any Christian that you know live according to strict ancient Jewish cultural laws? Of course, none do. The entirety of Christianity chooses not to follow Old Testament law. All Christians pick and choose rules of morality from the Old Testament. They use their hearts, minds, and spirits to make these choices. The Old Testament is not and has never been a strict source for morality in the Christian religion. Christian leaders throughout history have made this clear.

Most prominently, when Christians condemn homosexuality, they fall back on the words of Paul in the New Testament. Paul addressed the issue of homosexual acts when he admonished people for many different kinds of hurtful, selfish, sinful behaviors. But maybe Paul wasn't condemning anyone for actually loving another person, even if it's an awkward and strange manner for some people to witness. Maybe he wasn't urging anyone to judge and condemn people for who they wanted to be with romantically. Perhaps Paul was addressing a much larger issue for all people: lust and selfishness, the symptoms of which were promiscuity and adultery. Maybe his goal was to condemn people who did *not* love and respect each other.

Paul condemned the harm that promiscuity and adultery brought to all relationships, no matter what combinations of the sexes were involved. In Romans 1:25–27 he condemned the manner in which people handled their sexual impulses. He condemned people who "worshipped and served the things God created instead of the Creator himself." People were worshipping and serving their lust for the human body, so Paul directed his disappointment at people who "indulged in sex" and "burned with lust." He was making a profound point about our sexuality, that it can be harmful when love is absent. Paul ultimately wanted people to experience the beauty that comes from a focus on the divine love of our Creator, even within the context of our sexual relationships.

In 1 Corinthians 6:9–10 and 1 Timothy 1:10 Paul listed a myriad of ways in which people turned to harmful, unholy, unloving sexual choices, and he directed his disappointment at all people who were guilty of such behavior, regardless of their sexual orientation. Amid the long list of sins that he described, people who "practice homosexuality" are certainly included, but these verses were anything but a strict condemnation of a particular group of people with a particular sexual orientation. It was a condemnation of all people whose sexual practices lead to harm.

If we are to learn anything from these chapters we must read them with an appreciation for context. Paul had nothing bad to say in any those verses about a beautiful lifestyle where a woman loves a woman intimately and selflessly. He wasn't admonishing the lifestyle of two men whose relationship is based in sincerity and love. Paul let people know that lust and selfishness can bring terrible consequences into anyone's life! They can destroy relationships because they're *not* based in love. Paul was talking about people *not* loving one another!

Every adult should understand the emotional pitfalls and negative consequences that our sexual desires can bring into our lives. Our sexual desires and actions can lead us down destructive paths, no matter what sexual organs are involved. Our desires can cause deep emotional harm to ourselves, our partners, and people around us. This is a big issue for humanity. It has always been and it always will be. It certainly was in Paul's time as he addressed people in Greek and Roman culture. And today it's a big issue for us. Paul's words in these sections can be read as a commentary on people who submit to selfish pleasure, people who don't respect or cherish each other, and end up bringing a lot of pain and ugliness into their lives.

Most cultures, until recently, have lived in fear of complex topics regarding sexuality because they don't know how to face it. They don't know how to resolve it. These Bible verses could be read literally and in isolation, with little consideration for context. And of course, heterosexuals can read them that way and piously assume that these verses don't apply to them. We *can* read them that way, but that's often how hasty judgments are made, without appreciation for the largeness of the issues. Making matters worse, it's hard to accept that people are different from us. This is especially hard for proud men who feel that their masculinity is being threatened. And it's not surprising that the Christian church has condemned homosexuality for centuries, because it's men who have governed its institutions.

Unfortunately, unlike some innocuous topics that various cultures have mishandled, the poor handling of sexuality and gender issues has often resulted in shockingly terrible treatment of humans. It's resulted in violence, shame, and exclusion often because men don't know how to handle it with maturity. This is one of the awful tragedies of Christianity. So perhaps today we owe it to humanity and to God to look at these issues with maturity.

Questions regarding sexuality can be confounding and are not easily resolved, but they are our reality as God's creation. They are especially confounding for the people who wrestle with them in their hearts, minds, bodies, and spirits. Unfortunately the Christian church has often made life much worse for the people who wrestle with them, those people whose identities don't properly align with simplistic norms and expectations. Countless numbers of humans have lived with emotional darkness, hurt, shame, fear, and violence because of the shortcomings of Christian leaders. So the question must be asked, has the church whiffed on the issue of homosexuality? Was Paul issuing judgment on God's creation, or was he identifying selfish and careless behaviors that can harm each of us? Was Paul being so simpleminded that he rendered condemnation on a particular set of sexual orientations, or was he addressing the state of every person's heart, mind and spirit?

The temptations of sexual promiscuity and adultery are issues for every human to face. Perhaps that's why Paul addressed them—because they cause problems for so many people. And perhaps there is much more to this discussion than what the church has often assumed. Paul even said in Galatians 3:28, "There is no longer Jew or Gentile, slave or free, male and female." The challenge of following and becoming like Christ is not about race, social status, sexual orientation, or gender identification. It's about something far more expansive: love and what results from the love that we extend to others.

Never forget what Jesus said in Matthew 7:18: "A good tree can't produce bad fruit, and a bad tree can't produce good fruit." Perhaps Paul was not condemning humans who commit to homosexual relationships in love, sincerity, and the production of good *fruit*. And perhaps Paul's words should speak to anyone who engages in any sexual activity out of lust and selfishness. A heterosexual, homosexual, transsexual, or any other *sexual* who bases their relationship in good fruit—love, joy, peace, patience, kindness, goodness, faithfulness, gentleness, self-control—will not produce bad fruit. Paul made this clear in Galatians 5:22–23.

Maturity in Us

Questions over the Bible's historical accuracy, language, moral relativism, and homosexuality are difficult for many Christians to face. This is often because we weren't taught to face them. We were mostly told to accept institutional answers. But if we don't face them, the foundations of our faith may never become solid. They might always remain closer to paper-thin.

We can spot a paper-thin belief system by how fiercely it responds to a threat that might tear it apart. That's because paper-thin belief systems know they are vulnerable. And we don't like to feel vulnerable. So quite commonly, we attack the threats. But if we were truly mature, we would not fear or vilify threats; rather, we would spend our efforts coming to terms with why our faith is vulnerable and why parts of our foundations are so shaky. Perhaps occasionally we would even *allow* our faith to be torn so we could start building a more solid, mature faith.

Author and philosopher Pete Rollins told a story of a religious leader who shared his belief that "most people don't want to think for themselves . . . basically that people are sheep." Rollins identified this leader's perspective as pessimistic. He did acknowledge that not everyone is ready to think completely for themselves on every complex topic, but he also said that in the right environment people can learn to break free of this sheep mentality.[13] And isn't the right environment one that's open, loving, inclusive, absent of judgment, and grounded in God's expansiveness? Never forget how Paul described the love that Christ showed: "how wide, how long, how high, and how deep" (Ephesians 3:18).

This human experience is far from perfect. We all get things wrong, just like the church has gotten things wrong and done things wrong countless times over the centuries. We are all prone to reaching convoluted conclusions. Our minds can get wrapped up in our smallness, resentment, egos, and selfish ambitions. We are all prone to this when we carry the baggage of our humanity and sin. But each of us can step forward in maturity. Pope Francis said,

"Everyone must find Him in his or her own way. God cannot be found through hearsay, nor can you pay to encounter Him. It is a personal journey, and we must meet Him personally."[14]

This is a beautiful statement from the Pope, the most prominent leader in all of Christianity. It's a mature statement. His words may have been stated within the context of institutional Catholicism, but they extend to all aspects of our spiritual journeys. They acknowledge our free will and the gift of choice that God provides us.

How do you define spiritual maturity? How will you approach your faith? These are questions we can ask ourselves every single moment of every single day. This is the great gift that God gave us.

15. PRACTICE

D r. Martin Luther King, Jr. said, "One of the great tragedies of life is that men seldom bridge the gulf between practice and profession, between doing and saying."[1]

As a Navy helicopter pilot I flew the CH-46 Sea Knight. It was a massive, industrial beast—the size of a school bus but with two massive sets of rotors on top. The amount of fuel, oil, and hydraulic lines running inside the skin of the aircraft would boggle the average person's mind. Its two big engines cranked out over 1,200 horsepower each and shaft speeds of 6,000 rpm. Then two huge transmissions spun the rotors fast enough to lift that 18,000-pound machine, plus another 5,000 pounds of cargo up into the air with ease. These machines produced deafening amounts of noise. Extreme heat, pressure, and vibration needed to be expertly maintained and monitored if people expected to return safely from their flights, much less complete their missions. When you came upon one of these machines, you were compelled to have a serious amount of respect for them. And fear.

I completed two wartime deployments to the Middle East as a Sea Knight aircraft commander, and I learned that I needed every person in my crew to be at the top of their game. If we weren't, there were many instances where we might not have completed our mission, or worse, we might not have returned to land safely. Each of us was human and prone to mistakes, and making mistakes while operating those massive machines could've yielded terrible consequences. We had to cover for each other, keep each other sharp, and lift each other up when someone slipped or made a mistake. We all needed to have a positive effect on each other if we were to succeed at our job and in some cases simply survive.

I learned quickly that telling people to prepare for flights, investigate the mission details, check maintenance records, get enough rest the night before, and maintain a keen sense of awareness during these flights was a limited way to influence people. And reminding them that our helicopters were dangerous didn't help either. Words just didn't go very far. The development of my beliefs regarding preparation and professionalism was a necessary step in my maturity as a leader, but it happened early on, and it really wasn't difficult. Like I said, the amount of fear and respect you gain while standing in the vicinity of one of these machines quickly made you consider the manner in which you approached your work. So at some point, I realized if I was going to be an effective and successful aircraft commander, I had to mature beyond my beliefs and show that I actually embodied them. It was the only way to have a positive influence on my coworkers, the people who would keep me safe when I made a mistake. They needed to see that I was *doing* all my preparations and *exhibiting* the highest levels of professionalism. That was the way to ensure that we returned safely from every flight and accomplished every mission.

Habits

So far this book has been a lot of talk. That's because this is where so many of us need to start. As individuals, as communities, and as a culture we need to start talking about important things, like what really matters to us. Who do we want to be, and how do we want to live? What role does our faith play in our lives? These discussions matter. But at some point, they need to turn into action or they will have been just a lot of talk. There comes a time when we must take ownership of the things that matter to us and move toward practice.

The practice of nurturing meaningful living and spiritual growth can be related to a diet. The diet industry is a 200-billion-dollar marketing and sales industry.[2] Unfortunately, what so many people often buy into are quick-fix weight loss programs that were developed for someone else. They might work for us for a little while, but eventually they lose their effectiveness. What we need to remember, but what none of us ever want to hear, is that healthy living requires a significant commitment. It requires us to discover our individual needs and tendencies, to learn what techniques work for us, and then to commit to the effort of changing our habits. This is no small undertaking.

Knowledge of our caloric intake will not, by itself, change what we ingest. Buying healthier foods at the grocery store will not, by itself, change our bodies. And subscriptions to diet regimens will not, by themselves, change our eating habits. Ultimately, we must do the hard work of overcoming harmful habits and developing good ones. And we must overcome harmful habits in environments where unhealthy meal options are far more convenient and often cheaper than healthy ones. This is not easy.

The challenges of meaningful living and spiritual growth are similar to those of healthy living today. There are many paths toward healthier living, but none are easy in our culture. And certainly none will be achieved passively. Voices at every turn try to convince us to quit. But we can make progress if we choose to commit ourselves a little bit every day. This helps us develop mind-sets that reject unhealthy choices and seek healthy ones, and it helps us to gradually lose bad habits as we form good ones.

Meditation & Mindfulness

A great place to start bringing our faith into our lives is meditation and mindfulness. These practices help clear our minds by detaching from all the thoughts and emotions swirling in our heads. They don't rid us of harmful and negative thoughts, but they help us move beyond them. This isn't always easy because these kinds of thoughts are fostered in our culture. But we can make progress with just a little bit of time and effort every day. Even just a few minutes of quiet meditation at home, in the car, or on a park bench can help point our minds toward good things. Think of it. Five minutes when our day starts and when it comes to a close can help train our brains to move beyond negative and stressful thoughts and hold on to positive ones. And good thoughts can eventually translate into better actions—better responses in our interactions with other people, better efforts in our relationships and communities, better goals, and better experiences during both success and hardship.

There are hundreds of books, programs, and apps available to help you develop the practice of meditation. The widespread selection can be overwhelming, but all you have to do is try one. Work on one program for a few days or weeks. Try it in the comfort of your home, and try to it outside, on a walk or in a park. See where it takes you. See how valuable it can be. See if it brings good things into your life. And whenever you're ready, dive deeper into more expansive and demanding meditation exercises.

Learn

We live in a world with extraordinary access to information, and we therefore have an incredible opportunity to learn what other people have discovered about the Bible and the Christian faith. Until recently the only people who had this kind of access were the ones who attended an educational institution that specialized in biblical training. And a few hundred years before that people could only learn about the Bible from their religious leaders. Bibles may not have been printed in their language, nor were they widely available to be viewed. Today, however, we can read books and commentaries from the world's greatest and the most obscure theologians. We can learn what all kinds of religious leaders have to say about our faith. It's all online, right there for the taking. So if the Bible—this ancient collection of holy texts—is important to you, seek to learn more about it. Read commentaries that were written throughout history. Look at publications and periodicals that are produced today. Watch videos and listen to podcasts on faith, spirituality, and the Bible. Study it for yourself and allow it to enter your life.

Prayer

Prayer is another exercise that can help your faith be more present in your life. And like meditation, there is more guidance on how to pray than you could ever consume. One place to start is simply saying the word *God*. Just say it a few times. Don't worry about what comes next. You might not be ready to open your heart and mind to God right away, and that's fine. But saying that word can connect you with something expansive. It can train your heart, mind, and spirit to think about the divine and eventually to dwell with it.

Or your prayer could just involve listening and wondering. It could be sitting quietly and keeping an open mind about God. And when you're ready to step up your prayer practice to something deeper and more expansive, seek guidance from someone who does have experience with it, or look to books and publications, or join a group that prays together regularly. If God is real, and if God knows you, and if you hope to live someday in a more profound union with God, then it's time to communicate with God. It's time to connect. And just saying that word can start a conversation, because a conversation with the divine doesn't require an extensive or perfectly articulated introduction.

Rituals

Get yourself to a spiritual service if you think that could help you achieve a deeper and more disciplined spiritual life. As critical as I have been in this book about the Christian church, it remains the central place for Christ-centered spiritual practice. Hopefully aspects of it will change in the coming years to create a more inviting and engaging experience for our population, but the weekly rituals that occur in church services are intended to foster a profound experience with our Creator. Group prayer, lectures, classes, presentations, artistic performances, music, silence, readings, lectures, and sacraments like the Eucharist (or communion) and confession can all help us grow with purpose in our faith.

So get yourself to a church service if you think it can help you grow a deeper and more disciplined faith. Understand also that you might never find a service that perfectly matches your preferences on any of these rituals. But do go if you think they can help you to grow.

The Practice of Goodness

Meditation, prayer, and rituals are great steps in enhancing spiritual discipline. But these activities are most often done apart from our everyday lives, tasks, and interactions. Most people would never meditate or visibly engage in prayer at the office. Nor should they. Those activities are normally done privately or in the setting of a religious service. But church services only take up about an hour every week, so what about all the other hours?

Here's a possibility: work to be mindful of your faith in the regular, everyday events of your life. Turn your mind toward the divine during the activities that you already do regularly: working, cooking, cleaning, exercising, driving, shopping, watching movies, and listening to music and podcasts. Often times, Christians feel pressure to listen only to *Christian* music, to read *Christian* books, or to watch *Christian* programs. That's fine. But they aren't the extent of our spiritual experiences. Whatever you listen to, read, watch or access, do it for *good* reasons. Watch a movie that helps you think about *good* things. Listen to music and podcasts that open your mind to deeper and more profound thoughts. Whatever your job is, while you're working to collect a paycheck, think also about how you can serve others. When you donate money or volunteer in your community, think about why it's good to do so and whom you are helping.

Look around your office or your neighborhood and find someone who needs help with something, and then lend a hand. Think of all those miracles Jesus did for people—healing the crippled, the blind, the chronically ill, and lepers, even bringing dead people back to life. Why did he do those things? Because it helped people. It served them. It brought beauty and joy into their lives.

When you buy groceries for your family or your housemates, think about how you are doing something good for them. And whether you buy food for an eight-person household or if you live alone, think about buying a little something extra for someone who could use it. This small act of generosity can bring so much beauty into the world. It can literally change someone's day. Or when you're out buying coffee, a sandwich, or a smoothie, look around the room and pay someone else's bill. It's a small expense, but it says something huge about how important goodness is to you.

A lot of church leaders say that the path toward God is church, the regular ritual of worship and recognition of the supremacy of God. They're not wrong. It's one path, but it's not the only path. At least, that's what the man at the center of the Christian religion kept saying. Jesus said it dozens of times—*follow* me, *believe* in me, have *faith* in me. These statements acknowledge his spiritual supremacy, but they also focus on what we think, do, and bring into our lives. The act of thinking *good* thoughts, doing *good* deeds, and bringing *goodness* into the world . . . that's literally what our faith can be. The act of making our lives into something beautiful, impactful, and profound is a real path toward knowing and living in union with our Creator. This is the *way* of Christ. It is a way to an *eternal* kind of life, the kind of life that so many of us desire.

To Change One's Mind

Don't underestimate what happens to you when you experience God through *good* things. It can be a profound experience, and it can change you. We know from the study of neuroscience that our brains change as we form good habits. Those of us in the faith refer to it as a change in our hearts and spirits. Some Christians prefer the term *transformation*. And many Christians ascribe this process to the work of the Holy Spirit—the spirit of God that lives in us. Whatever we call it, we can experience life on a more deep and profound level when we commit to it.

There is a word in our English Bibles that has kept the focus of some people's faith very small. It has failed to encourage people to expand their hearts, minds, and spirits into something more profound. That word is *repent*, and it undersells a major concept that the man at the center of the Christian religion was teaching people two thousand years ago. Read what Father Richard Rohr said about it:

> Jesus' first recorded word in at least two Gospels, *metanoia*, is unfortunately translated with the moralistic, churchy word 'repent.' The word quite literally means 'change' or even more precisely, 'Change your minds!' (Mark 1:15; Matthew 4:17). Given that, it is quite strange that the religion founded in Jesus' name has been so resistant to change and has tended to love and protect the past and the status quo much more than the positive and hopeful futures that could be brought about by people agreeing to change. Maybe that is why our earth is so depleted and our politics are so pathetic. We have not taught a spirituality of actual change or growth."[3]

It's unfortunate that the English translation of the Greek word *metanoia* by European men hundreds of years ago has kept us so focused on the limited activity of admitting shortcomings. Christian leaders in the English-speaking world have harped about repentance and confession for centuries. Religious institutions have practically built an industry on the mandated admission of sin and its accompanying guilt. But it's interesting that the master of life was not concerned with how sorry we feel about anything. He never told anyone to keep a tally of their poorest behaviors. And he never told anyone to apologize for how they were created—sinful and imperfect. Rather, he encouraged people to move forward into a life of beauty, peace, and positive impact. The act of confessing or repenting does take effort and it can have good benefits. Sometimes it helps us to swallow our pride. But the act itself can happen in a moment, and the greater point is to start moving beyond it, and to allow the experience of God to change and transform our lives.

Patience

Change rarely happens fast for us. The external world can change rapidly. Weather, stock markets, and contagious illnesses can change the world quickly, but humans do not change quickly. Certainly, our minds are not easily changed. That's one reason why there is so much fuss and exasperation on social media. How much effect *can* a typed, two-dimensional, argumentative posting on a computer screen really have on a person?

As you digest meaningful topics, you must spend time with them, allow their insights to seep into your heart and mind. Give these topics time to swirl around the rarely accessed depths of your spirit. Meditate with them. If you are someone who prays, then of course pray over them. Ponder meaningful topics when you eat, cook, clean, drive, watch or listen to media, sit on a bus or a train, sit in an airport, run, walk, bike, lie in bed waiting to fall asleep, or wake in the morning before you get out of bed. The more you bring them into your life, the more you allow them to change and transform you.

In contemplating any important topic, you may have to develop the discipline of ignoring distractions. Understand that we often stare at electronic screens, for example, to avoid the depths of our existence. The silence of our often-ignored depths can be terrifying. So it's often easier to avoid them by being mindlessly entertained. But I encourage you to give silence a chance. Learn to appreciate it and grow in it. Find yourself and the divine in it.

Finally, gear your actions and behaviors toward *good* things. It's profound that when we practice our faith by doing good things for others, both we and the others are affected. It's like a doubling of healing and growth. And it really is profound. Our hearts swell. Our spirits soar. Seems like a good case for faith today.

16. CONNECTION AND COMMUNITY

There is an epidemic in our culture. It started to take its toll on our population long before COVID-19, and it has spread much wider. It's an epidemic of loneliness and separation. It's everywhere. It affects all age groups, and it seems to hit the younger generations hardest. There are many reasons why it's spread, but fortunately we have weapons to fight against it. These weapons are connection and community.

One of the most beautiful things about the human experience is our connection with other people. Feeling connected might be the deepest and most profound thing we ever feel. Our healthiest relationships are defined by strong connections. Our bonds with friends, family members, children, and lovers are rooted in deep connections. And of course the same is true for our connection to our Creator.

Contrarily, we all understand how awful it feels when we are disconnected and isolated. Philosopher Jean Vanier said, "Loneliness is a feeling of not being part of anything, of being cut off. . . . It is a taste of death."[1] Loneliness is one of the great threatening darknesses of our time. Loneliness and separation are awful experiences, and I believe they are closely related to the concept of hell because they are the opposite of the incredible, connected, eternal life that Jesus spoke of. So I propose that we start driving them out.

Younger Generations

For centuries churches have served as places of connection and community in Western culture. With the continued diminishing relevance of organized religion, however, that is largely not the case today. Hopefully many churches will consider how they can adapt and transform so they can remain dependable, relevant centers of community. And as they do work through these considerations, an important question to ask is how they will embrace the personality of the younger generations. Many churches might not want to cater to younger crowds today, but if they don't, the trend of diminishing church attendance will leave them with little hope to remain prolific or even functional. These statements do not originate from pessimism or resentment. They are grounded in reality. The numbers tell us so. The Christian church at large has experienced a notable declining trend since the latter part of last century, and younger generations are less likely to associate with them with every passing decade. The writing is on the wall. If church organizations want to be healthy, or if they just want to continue to exist, they must consider the people who could support their organizations in the future—this generation of young adults.

Younger generations might be more interested in practices that help them learn to be present amid all the raucous and distraction of the twenty-first century rather than ones that merely focus on worship. They might be more interested in engaging discussions about the example of Jesus and how it pertains to their lives rather than simplistic lectures about how great he is. They might benefit from activities that connect them with other people, both where they can be supported and where they can support others. They might experience something more profound in popular music and art than in aged hymns and praise-our-superhero music. They might be more interested in getting out and doing something, like a service project where they focus on God's creation, rather than sitting through a church service that espouses doctrine and the *right* beliefs. More than anything, they might just want to sit at a table and share a meal. Eating together can be a profound act of connection. Or they might not want to do any of these things. The point is that *they* are viewed as important, that *they* are engaged, and that *they* learn how to have a life that is beautiful, impactful, and profound, just like the one Christ lived.

Younger generations might also want to spend time discussing what it means to live well in this age of shallowness and self-centeredness. Renowned pastor and author Tim Keller saw this potential and said, "I think these younger Christians are the vanguard of some major new religious, social, and political arrangements that could make the older form of culture wars obsolete."[2] His statement is cause to be optimistic. It's also reason to start anticipating and even demanding that changes happen within corporate Christianity. And again, this is where the master of life stands out as an example worth considering. His words and his actions serve as a profound model for our movement into a new church culture.

Some number of people in the younger generations will want to engage traditional practices like communion, confession, and the recitation of creeds, but the expectation that church activities should include these practices is certainly in question. Today there are more forms of worship than we can count. For this reason, we can equate them to books on a bookshelf. Picture a wall full of books. Thousands of books. All different colors, sizes, publication dates, authors, languages, subjects, etc. The form of service that a church employs on Sunday morning is just one book. One among thousands. There are more forms and versions than we could ever imagine. But what if we considered other books—other forms.

What if there was a long period of quiet meditation on the Creator of the universe? What if there was no sermon at all, but a question-and-answer session with your pastor? What if there was a discussion on the comparison of our lives to that of Christ? What if there was a listening session where we talked about how various *non-*

churchy songs connect us with the Spirit of God? What if your preacher invited local experts to speak on the wonders of science, psychology, or nature? What if a guest preacher from another denomination or another religion visited and presented on the tenants and value of their beliefs and practices. What if your congregation just met outside and had a picnic? Or met at a playground to clean up the trash? All these activities can direct our hearts toward God. And they can all help us learn to love God and our neighbor.

One of Many

Many Christians cherish their form of worship. Many of these forms have also endured through the ages, so there's no need to abandon what's worked for hundreds of years . . . if it works for people today. But when a church faces dwindling attendance, might it be a good idea to try another form? Another book? Remember what Christ said about weekly spiritual ritual: "The Sabbath was made to meet the needs of people, and not people to meet the requirements of the Sabbath" (Mark 2:27).

Don't be afraid to grab a different book off the shelf. Or write one of your own. What is there to be afraid of? Does your God-given conscience not guide you? Is the goodness of God not written on your heart? Obviously you don't want to grab a book titled *Personal Destruction and Bad Habits.* Make sure to grab or write one that's based in good things. As long as they point to something *good*—good fruits and good connections—then God calls them *good.* As C. S. Lewis said, "The perfect church service would be one we were almost unaware of. Our attention would have been on God." Our attention can be on God in all kinds of different activities and in all parts of our lives. And isn't that the goal?

Adaptations and transformations of services don't have to be a rejection of God, Jesus, or Scripture. They are simply a different way to connect with them. These changes could actually help many people better connect with them. If you can open your mind to it, you might even feel excitement about the future of the church and the place it could have in our culture. The Christian church could have a hand in raising people out of disconnectedness and separation. It could embody the incredible example of generous, inclusive love that Jesus so vividly gave us. Vast numbers of people have left the church, but if they can be served again, some number of them might someday return with vigor. Like Tim Keller said, some of them might be the vanguard of something profound. Many of them might also want to return to traditional practices and services. But this can only happen once our communities of faith figure out how to serve them. Otherwise, what reason do they have to return?

Good Connections

One good way to serve people and foster connection and community is by throwing parties. Sometimes we throw a party to celebrate a great achievement or a birthday. Sometimes we throw a party to welcome people as they join a community or to honor them as they depart. Other times we throw a party just because we want to be together. Sometimes it's just a good idea to connect.

At our parties we stand together over food and drink. We share our stories and we relate. We talk, laugh, and listen. We connect. We play music. Sometimes we dance. Sometimes we just listen and feel. The great thing is that when we throw parties, we don't accomplish anything. We aren't completing tasks. We aren't being productive. We simply come together, and we become a community.

You might also feel compelled to hold an event that does more than just get people together. You may want to invite people to dig into discussion or investigate a particular practice. One way to make an event more meaningful for people is to add meaningful activities: live music, presentations on important topics, and purposeful discussion. This could be a great way to provide content for people's hearts, minds, and spirits. Music that articulates our deep questions or settles our souls can absolutely be meaningful, especially when the experience is shared with others. Presentations on culture, science, art, relationships, psychology, social media, community needs, Scripture, prayer, habits, spiritual practice, and a host of other important topics might draw people in, give them a reason to come. And discussions where people can search and express what's in their hearts, minds, and spirits could even give people a reason to return.

Events like this could be held in our homes with a few people or at a venue with hundreds of people. They won't satisfy everyone's deep questions on every topic, but they could be a way to create connections and form community. For someone who holds the Christian faith close but does not attend church, this could be a way to enter into something meaningful. And for someone who is mature in their faith and finds value in traditional worship services, it could be a way to make new connections and form a broader community. And for anyone else, it could just be an interesting and engaging experience. Not everyone will enter with the same beliefs or form the same conclusions, and that's a beautiful thing. God grants us the freedom to be ourselves in our search for connection, community, and spirituality.

Meet

For centuries in Western civilization, churches were the center of neighborhood communities. If there was to be a community gathering, it was often held at the local church. If people needed any sort of help, the first place they would go was the church. But things have changed. Millions of people refuse to turn to these institutions for community or assistance. *Facts & Trends* recently published an article that states between 6,000 and 10,000 churches close every year.[3] More conservative estimates put that number between 3,850 and 7,700.[4] Regardless of what the exact number is, the trend of churches closing in America is consistent and it's pervasive. And there is reason to believe that the effects of COVID-19 will accelerate the number of church closings.[5] Yet a majority of Americans still identify with the Christian religion. So what's the problem? Why can't churches keep people's interest? Why can't churches become an important, relevant, and meaningful force in people's lives?

As I've stated many times previously in this book, one big reason might be because the message of the church Christian does not matter *in* people's lives. And if we ever want it to, maybe we should look closer at all the places where people spend their lives. Reggie McNeal reminded us that "Jesus' strategy was to go where people were already hanging out. He went to weddings, parties, lakeshores, and religious feast-day celebrations." [6] He even brought the wine!

And when we meet people there, we point our discussion and our efforts right at our lives. The questions we ask, the topics we bring up, they can start right where people are living. Because that's what matters. How we live is important—how we take care of each other, how we grow and mature, how we care for this earth. Why wouldn't we start there?

Here are some questions that could do a lot of good for people:

When do we experience peace in our lives?
When does anxiety overwhelm us?
How do we overcome jealousy?
Why is there resentment in our relationships?
How do we get over an addiction?
What does it mean to be humble?
What does it mean to be beautiful?
How do we define success?
What are some causes that we could support?
How can we have a more positive impact in our workplace?
How can we take care of our neighborhood?
What can I do to help others who are arguing?
How do I react when someone wants to argue with me?
How can I help people feel loved and valued?
What does it mean to have faith today?
Does any of this faith and spirituality stuff even matter?

The questions go on and on. They begin with our lives, and they grow outward, toward the world around us. God is with us through the journey. Jesus' words and example guide us. And at some point we start actually serving God and this creation without even knowing it. Just like the greatest commandment in Matthew 22, we love God and our neighbor. But we don't have to start with exclusive doctrine, or systematic theology, or the abstract significance of events that happened two thousand years ago.

The incredible thing is that all kinds of people can ask and discuss these questions together: young people, middle-aged people, senior citizens, millennials and boomers, people who speak English properly and people who struggle with the English language, people with lots of money and people with no savings at all, people who practice an exotic religion and people who practice no religion, people who think they might be living right and people who know they are living wrong, spiritually minded people, atheists, and agnostics, people who are just slightly curious and people who want to dig deeper, people with light or dark or medium-shade skin tones, and anyone else who stands inside or outside these descriptions. ANYONE! These questions aren't about exclusivity, proper spiritual beliefs, or being "right." They're simply about what's important and good today. That's what we can connect over. And that's how we can form new and profound communities.

Connection and community are so badly needed today. And what are we, as Christ followers, doing to foster it? Are we demanding that people subscribe to a belief system before we connect with them? Should they sign a paper before they join our club? Are we inviting them into our church buildings with the assumption that they will get excited about our singular form of worship? If we are, we shouldn't be surprised when nobody new shows up. And we shouldn't be surprised when our church communities keep aging, shrinking, and disappearing.

So what are we doing to foster connection and community? Are we fighting loneliness and separation? Are we helping young adults learn how to live with depth and meaning? Are we helping people experience God in the context of their lives? Are we asking good questions and willing to listen to other people's answers? If we're not, what's the point of any of this? Why did God even create us? Why not just drop our souls right into heaven, if that's really where God wants us to be? And why did Jesus waste his time, effort, sweat, and blood showing and teaching people how to live the most beautiful life ever?

Think about the needs of your community and how the manifestation and practice of your faith can affect it. Think about connections and the good that it can do for people. And think big! Don't assume that the *way* of Christ is just for churchgoers. And don't assume that there is just one way to do church. Grow your practices in goodness, and you will find a community that is beautiful, impactful, and profound.

17. MORE

Jesus said, "I am the way, the truth, and the life" (John 14:6).

It was the afternoon of June 28, 2005. I had one more year left in the Navy and I was teaching at a university on Long Island, New York. Classes were done for the summer, grades were turned in, the students went home, and I had a few weeks of flexibility to start preparing for my upcoming career change to become a musician in New York City. I would be taking all kinds of advanced guitar lessons and making as many contacts as possible in the music industry. That afternoon I had taken the train into the city, and then a subway up to 86th Street on the Upper West Side. I popped out into the beautiful summer air and started walking to the apartment of a really stellar jazz guitarist who was giving me private lessons. Things were going great. My skills were improving. My network was growing. And then my cell phone rang.

It was the regional Casualty Assistance Office. They were calling about an assignment to spend time with a family of a Navy officer who was missing. This officer was a SEAL and had been in a firefight with Taliban troops in a remote part of Afghanistan earlier that day, but no one knew where he was or if he was alive. The assignment was to notify the family, stay with them throughout the day, support

them, and be a liaison between them and the Navy. I knew exactly
what it meant. It meant I would spend all day every day out at their
house until their son was found. And if it turned out their son was
killed, I would spend the next few weeks with them. It could take up
almost all of my free time. I felt awful for that family, but I argued not
to take it. I told the woman on the phone that she needed to give this
assignment to someone else. I had just set out in my plans to prepare
for a new career.

For a minute, I tried to squirm my way out of it, but finally I
succumbed. There were only a handful of other qualified people in
the area to do the job, and it was my turn. And I'm so glad that it was,
because that assignment turned out to be the most profound, important, and rewarding thing I ever did in the service.

I spent the next three weeks out at their house serving as a
support system. I relayed questions about angel flights, the military
transport flights that returned bodies home from overseas. I helped
make funeral arrangements. I was able to clear up questions about
their son's belongings and the awkward task of handling life insur-
ance. I drove with the family down to Dover Air Force Base in
Delaware to bring their son's body, in a flag-draped casket, back to
their hometown. I facilitated visits from other Navy SEALs and
people who'd worked with their son who wanted to grieve with the
family. I met with the funeral director to coordinate the military
honors that their son would receive. I communicated with the
veterans cemetery on Long Island where their son would be buried. I
went to the wake. I shook hands and shared condolences with what
seemed like a thousand friends and relatives. And most importantly, I
spent a lot of time in their house. For hours on end I would sit and
talk with the parents, sibling, cousins, aunts, uncles, and childhood
friends. We talked about life in the service, training, deploying, and
traveling. They wanted to know more about what it was like for their
loved one to be in the military. And more than anything, they wanted
to tell me about him. They wanted me to know what a huge place
Michael had in their life.

They told me about his courage and how he stood up for kids at school who were being harassed. They told me about how he once saved someone's life at the beach where he lifeguarded but that he didn't want to tell anybody about it. They told me what a relentless athlete and inspiring teammate he was in high school. They told me how hard he prepared for his Navy training and how he could have gone to law school but instead committed to the service, perhaps the most dangerous and demanding organization in the service—the SEALs. They told tell me how much he loved the guys in his SEAL Team, and how important it was to help them stay safe and alive through all their dangerous missions. And they shared the deep anguish they felt when we all finally learned that Michael was killed in those remote mountains of Afghanistan. They wanted to articulate the hole that was left in their lives. And over time, I began to feel that hole myself. I began to feel their loss with them. They had invited me into their family and showed me immense amounts of love, and they allowed me to experience something profound. That was the deep joy I had in serving them.

My service to them was important. It mattered, deeply. It had an impact. It brought them small moments of peace and levity. The immensity of this experience first became clear a few days after we learned of Michael's death. I had spent the day out at Michael's parents' house meeting with friends and family, and on the drive home that afternoon I cried. I cried because I had received their welcoming and love. And I felt their loss. It was just a fraction of the pain they felt, but it made me want to do everything in my power to help them. They became special to me. And they became the focus of my efforts that summer. They gave me such a gift, the love of their family and the story of their son.

I learned that Michael did everything in humility and that he was keenly focused, even as a child, to serve people, to lift them up and protect them. He seemed to have a profound effect on the people he encountered. He seemed to have an influence on people because they wanted to resemble him and live up to his example. And his actions touched people's hearts. I never even knew him. I just knew the hole that remained when he died, and it was an incredible example of who a person can be and the impact a person can have.

We learned later that Michael was ultimately killed because he stepped out into an open, unprotected area where he could get reception on his satellite phone. That was the only way to reach his base and request support for his struggling teammates. And that's when he was killed, when the enemy saw him exposed and fired on him. He sacrificed himself to request help for the guys he loved.

To learn about this event was no surprise to anyone who knew him, but it still hurt them deeply. It hurt to know that such a beautiful display of selflessness could also have such terrible consequences. But it had a profound influence on others. People celebrated his act of selflessness. Memorials were raised in his honor. Charity events were held in his name. Special workout regimens were named after him. Congress even awarded him the Medal of Honor, the highest honor a military member can receive. Michael's story affects people. It's powerful. It's impactful. It matters. Two movies were even made to tell the story of his selflessness. The time I spent with his family was the most rewarding and profound thing I ever did in the service. I learned about the power of selflessness. I saw it in someone else's life, and I had experienced it in my own.

What About Today?

Christians, or Christ *followers,* believe that Jesus is their Savior, that something extraordinary happened for their souls when he rose from the dead. Christians talk a lot about how God had him punished for our sins on the cross, how our sins are now forgiven, and how he was victorious over the grave. But these ideas are all conceptual. They are theological theories. They are important to many people, but they often have difficulty reaching into our lives. They are often too ethereal to touch us, too abstract to affect us.

Many Christians believe that these concepts *will* matter once their hearts stop beating and their brain waves stop pulsing. That can be a comforting thought. But what about today? What about right now? We are stuck in the present moment. We can't ever leave it. So does anything Jesus did matter in this moment?

Look at where you sit right now. Look at your circumstances and think about your next few tasks. Look at the people around you and think about the interactions you will have with them. How much does the notion that your soul is cleansed and that your sins are forgiven change these interactions? How much does the understanding that Jesus conquered the grave influence them? Look at your job, your relationships, your responsibilities, things you do in your free time, and the circumstances in your neighborhood. How much does the possession of a ticket to heaven change them? If a profound change does occur, then you are experiencing an eternal kind of life. But for many of us, these concepts don't reach us. It's nice to think that we'll end up in heaven, but it doesn't affect much that happens today.

Look at almost everything Christ said and see how it was a campaign to strive for a life that is beautiful, impactful, and profound. The Sermon on the Mount, the woman at the well, the calming of the seas, the Good Samaritan, the healing of the sick, the pulling of dead people back into this life, the meals he ate in people's homes, the feeding of the thousands, the scolding of the Pharisees, the pleading for people to change their lives, the command to love God and our neighbors, the insistence that we believe and trust in his *way* . . . it goes on and on. He was intent on showing people how to live. He was offering them *life*. Even in his torture and death, he offered us profound *life*. This is an aspect of the death and resurrection story that often gets overlooked in favor of abstract theological concepts and theories.

Many Christians consider Jesus to be far more significant than just a teacher and example. They pray to him as God, as a member of the trinity, and ask that he fill their hearts with joy, love, and peace. This is a wonderful spiritual practice to employ, but as Dr. Martin Luther King, Jr. said, "Prayer is a marvelous and necessary supplement of our feeble efforts, but it is a dangerous substitute."[1]

We must also be directly involved in the course of our lives. And with the profound and perfect example of Christ at the forefront of our minds, we can set a course for a beautiful life. So when we talk about Jesus, maybe sometimes we need to move beyond the concept that he fixes everything for us so that we can recognize more clearly how our lives can change today, right now, in the twenty-first century, when we allow his incredible example to guide us.

Not Shocked

Incredible depth and meaning can be found in the Easter story, but it does not exist entirely in Jesus' resurrection. His resurrection from death is a profound moment in his story. It was especially profound for the people who knew him. Jesus shocked the hell out of them when he showed up. He was their dear friend. He was their beloved rabbi—their teacher, healer, and protector. They watched him get battered, bruised, and bloodied. They watched his breathing stop. They buried him. So of course they were completely shocked and elated when he suddenly appeared in a locked room where they were hiding. They were freaked out. One of them didn't even believe it was happening (John 20).

But for many of us who read the Gospels, we experience very little shock and elation that Jesus came back to life. We are reading this story two thousand years later. We had no personal connection with the man. And consider another angle: of course he came back to life. He was God! We are told at the beginning and throughout those Gospel books that Jesus was God. As strange as this theory is, the Gospel writers made it abundantly clear that Jesus was God in some manner of being. People will disagree on the semantics of that concept, but we all can at least acknowledge that the Gospel authors tell us early and often that Jesus was God. Therefore, perhaps 21st-century readers should know that he was capable of a resurrection, especially after he raised those other people from the dead (Luke 7, Luke 8, John 11). If Las Vegas had odds on the likelihood of Jesus' resurrection, perhaps we all should have been ready to wager.

Shocked

The account of Jesus' death, on the other hand, offers all of us something that is profound for our lives today. There are more theories and opinions written on why Jesus died than we could ever read. There is so much metaphorical language in the New Testament describing its significance, it's easy to see how so many different theories have come up. Theories of substitutional atonement, where God absolutely had to punish somebody for all our badness, are accepted by many Christian sects but not all.[2] Theories on renewal and rebirth are also popular. Many people believe that Jesus was just obeying a command from his Father, who suddenly (somewhere between the last book of the Old Testament and the first book of the New Testament) felt that humans had to be punished for their evilness. There are metaphors that refer to life, death, worlds that arise after we've been dead for a while, heaven, hell, kingdoms, forgiveness, sins, glory, satan, angels, and a whole lot of references to ancient Jewish apocalyptic rhetoric. Perhaps all the conclusions over the various discussions, metaphors, and explanations of Easter exist because the biblical authors couldn't completely comprehend the precise, cosmic purpose and ramifications of Jesus' death and resurrection. Perhaps they, too, were grappling with its grand significance.

Matthias Henze and Peter Enns, both authors and Bible scholars, stated that these biblical authors were trying to "make sense"[3] and "work through"the significance of the "Jesus event" when they sat down to write their letters.[4] Maybe this is why some of them reached slightly different conclusions. Perhaps we humans cannot ever fully understand or at least agree on the comprehensive cosmic purpose and implications of Jesus' death and resurrection. But no matter where we land on our conclusions, there is something that any person can take from it today.

He Was Looking at Me

When someone attacks us with actions or words, we often resist. We push back. We defend ourselves. And we should. It's too easy for people to take advantage of us, and it happens too often. This fight response is warranted today. But might there be something *more* to our lives than that? Might there be something *more* than just self-preservation and self-importance?

The master of life must have known something significant because he didn't strike back. He didn't resist. His whole life on record was a model exhibit of bold and assertive confrontation of forces that harmed people's well-being. He protected them from storms. He healed them when they suffered. He intervened when authorities threatened to throw stones at someone as a punishment. He even brought a child back to life after her parents were crushed from the reality of her death. So why was he so meek at the end? Where was his focus? What was he thinking about? There must have been a significant reason why he kept receiving torture in grace and humility. This must be a massively important piece of his story.

Here's one possibility: he was looking at me. Maybe he was focused on showing me something profound for my life. Maybe by not resisting while he was dying, he was showing me a grand and impactful way to *live*. He didn't push back. He didn't fight. He didn't preserve himself. Neither did he avoid all that pain and torture. He stepped into it and felt every bit of it. He endured it and resisted self-preservation. The promotion of his own importance was absent from his behavior.

Why? Why did he sacrifice himself? Maybe in those moments he wanted to offer me the chance to learn how to live in profound beauty. Maybe he wanted me to have the perfect example of how I can live out every minute of this tedious, sometimes lonely, some-times painful, often disappointing life with real impact. This kind of behavior is influential. The act of selfless sacrifice does not go unno-ticed. It can't. It's too alarming, too beautiful, and too rare. It has a profound effect on us when we witness it. The act of sacrifice is based in humility and generosity. It possesses an element of perfection, and it feels eternal. It's based in pure love. It might be the ultimate manifestation of love. And Jesus handed the perfect example of it right to us, sort of like a gift. He offered himself as a perfect sacrifice in the ugliest, most unfair circumstances. Maybe he did this so we could know how to do the same in our lives, so that we could have this incredible truth at our fingertips.

The master of life knew we would learn about the profound significance of sacrifice to some degree. I certainly learned it to a degree when I became a father, and when I served as a Casualty Officer for the family of a fallen Navy SEAL. But Jesus also knew that we would often forget it. He knew that we would often be distracted by the temptation of our self-importance. He knew we would often get confused about what really matters in our lives. So he gave us a picture-perfect example. And he showed us very clearly that a beautiful and eternal life, one that is connected to God, is all about how we give our time, efforts, and resources to others. Selfless sacrifice. This is the *way* of Christ, and it is full of truth.

To use familiar terms within the Christian faith, Jesus' example could actually *save* us from the temptation to act selfishly in many instances. It could actually give us *new life* after we've made a habit of living in shallowness and smallness. When we turn our focus toward this kind of *life*, we might even feel *forgiven* for all the self-centeredness that we exhibited previously.

The perfect example of how to live, that is something we can carry and focus on every minute of our lives. It matters today. Right now. It matters in our relationships and our interactions with others. It matters in every decision we ever make. It can save us in upcoming moments if we hold it close to our hearts, minds, and spirits . . . if we make it part of our psyche . . . if we commit to it, if we believe in it, trust in it, and have faith in it!

This kind of faith could actually change our lives and the world around us.

What It's About

For me, this Christ-following stuff is not about transactions. It's not about feeling sorry to God about how bad I am. It's not about the status of my soul. It's not about needing some deity to suffer so I can enter the great resort in the sky after I stop breathing. It's not about poor old Jesus obeying some strange mandate from his Father to get tortured. It's not about God working out some abstract plan to fix us so some select number of us can be worthy enough to hang out with him. For me, this Christian faith is about a commitment to live the most beautiful life I could ever imagine. It's about the incredible experience of living in humility, sincerity, and generosity, and the impact that has on the people around me. It's about the profound act of serving others and sacrificing for them. And for me, this is the essence of my connection with God. This is how I can connect with my Creator every day of my life. This is also the purpose of my interactions with the Bible. That holy book can help me see my life with clarity. It can be a mirror that shows me how I can live a beautiful, God-fearing, Christ-following, impactful life. This is the Christian faith to me. It is not institutional. It is not doctrinal. It is not exclusive. It is not abstract. Nor is it required. It's my choice.

Loving sacrifice, the giving of ourselves, seems to be a forgotten concept in our culture. Think about what that says about our hearts. Unfortunately it's also often overlooked in our churches. How often are we giving away our time, efforts, and resources for the good of others? How often are we more concerned with what happens inside our church buildings than outside? And why are we so often more obsessed with making sure that God feels sufficiently adored than actually living out the *way* of Christ? We could benefit from spending a day or a week contemplating these questions. Perhaps we should spend every day contemplating them.

You may or may not be into this Christianity stuff, but when I spend time contemplating all of this, I feel something extraordinary. I feel something deep and expansive. It offers so much *more* than what my culture offers and so much *more* than what I hear a lot of churches preaching. The example of Jesus' life and death is perhaps the most profound thing I know. It exposes my pride. It floods my heart with humility, and it changes my psyche. It transforms me. It helps me see my life more clearly, and it helps me love the people around me better. Is that Jesus working in me? Or is it the Spirit of God? I have my opinions. But most importantly, what is it for you? Does any of this mean anything to you? Does it matter? Is it relevant in your life today?

As the master of life said, what do you say?

CONCLUSION

This book cannot answer everyone's questions about faith, spirituality, and theology. Some people will have even more questions than
before they starting reading it. If this describes you, don't be discouraged. As Jesus said often, "Don't be afraid!" There will always be
questions, and there will always be choices. The point of this book
was never to answer all your questions. The point was to present
questions, start discussions, and provide what are hopefully some
profound suggestions. At best, this book is a stepping-off point for
people who are ready to face some important questions about faith in
the twenty-first century.

I believe that vast numbers of people today are ready for a new
discussion about how faith can be present in their lives, and that they
want it to be relevant. I believe that many people who are part of the
church, many people who have left the church, and many other
curious people are thirsty for a discussion like this. And as we enter
these discussions, the way of Christ sure looks like a good option. A
commitment to his way could really change our lives. It can change
our communities. It could even change the world. After spending
years pouring over every word that Jesus said in the Gospels, I believe
that this was precisely his goal—to show us how to transform our

lives, relationships, and communities into something more beautiful, impactful, and profound. Because quite often we really need help with that, don't we?

This time we have on earth is so short. As the apostle James said, "Your life is like the morning fog—it's here a little while, then it's gone" (James 4:14). At some moment our hearts will stop pumping blood. Our brains waves will stop pulsing. And that's it. What happens after that? I don't know exactly. Nobody knows exactly. All I can do today is work toward a good life, one that produces good *fruit*, that is connected with my eternal Creator, who is in me and around me. And this is no small thing. The world is crying out for people who can do this. This is why I see an extraordinary opportunity for faith in the 21st-century.

Sincerely,

J. W.

NOTES

Introduction

1. Wil Gafney, "Womanist Midrash," *The Bible for Normal People*, podcast, episode 105, 4:00, October 27, 2019, https://thebiblefornormalpeople.podbean.com/e/episode-46-wil-gafney-womanist-midrash/.
2. Timothy Keller, *The Reason for God* (New York: Penguin Group, 2008), 4.

1. My 21st-Century Faith Experience

1. Jeffrey M. Jones, "U.S. Church Membership Down Sharply in Past Two Decades," Gallup.com, April 18, 2019, accessed November 2, 2020, https://news.gallup.com/poll/248837/church-membership-down-sharply-past-two-decades.aspx.

2. The Great Rejection

1. Jeffrey M. Jones, "Church Membership Down Sharply in Past Two Decades," https://news.gallup.com/poll/248837/church-membership-down-sharply-past-two-decades.aspx.
2. Barna Group, "Signs of Decline & Hope Among Metrics in Faith," Barna.com, March 4, 2020, https://www.barna.com/research/changing-state-of-the-church/.
3. Pew Research Center, "In U.S., Decline of Christianity Continues at Rapid Pace," PewForum.org, October 17, 2019, https://www.pewforum.org/2019/10/17/in-u-s-decline-of-christianity-continues-at-rapid-pace/.
4. Pew Research Center, "America's Changing Religious Landscape." PewForum.org, May 12, 2015, https://www.pewforum.org/2015/05/12/americas-changing-religious-landscape/.
5. Pew Research Center, "America's Changing Religious Landscape."
6. Pew Research Center, "In U.S., Decline of Christianity Continues at Rapid Pace."
7. Art Raney, Daniel Cox, and Robert P. Jones, "Searching for Spirituality in the U.S.: A New Look at the Spiritual but Not Religious," PRRI, November 6, 2017, https://www.prri.org/research/religiosity-and-spirituality-in-america/.
8. Brian McLaren, *The Secret Message of Jesus* (Nashville, TN: W Publishing Group, 2006), 83.
9. Pew Research Center, "America's Changing Religious Landscape."
10. Pew Research Center, "When Americans Say They Believe in God, What Do They Mean?" PewForum.org, April 25, 2018, https://www.pewfo-

rum.org/2018/04/25/when-americans-say-they-believe-in-god-what-do-they-mean/.

11. Reggie McNeal, *The Present Future: Six Tough Questions for The Church* (San Francisco: Jossey-Bass, 2003), 102.

12. McNeal, *The Present Future*, 4.

13. David Kinnaman and Gabe Lyons, *unChristian: What a New Generation Really Thinks about Christianity . . . and Why It Matters* (Grand Rapids, MI: Baker Books, 2007), 39.

14. Kinnaman and Lyons, *unChristian*, 39.

3. The Great Denial

1. McNeal, *The Present Future*, 7.

2. Jones, "U.S. Church Membership Down Sharply in Past Two Decades."

3. King, *Strength to Love*, (Philadelphia: First Fortress, 1981), 15.

4. McNeal, *The Present Future*, 11.

5. Keller, *The Reason for God*, 58.

6. Michael Lipka, "5 Facts About Religion in Canada," PewForum.org, July 1, 2019, https://www.pewresearch.org/fact-tank/2019/07/01/5-facts-about-religion-in-canada/;

   Pew Research Center, "Being Christian in Western Europe," PewForum.org, May 29, 2018, https://www.pewforum.org/2018/05/29/being-christian-in-western-europe/.

4. Void and Opportunity

1. "Postmodern," *Merriam-Webster.com Dictionary*, accessed May 13, 2020, https://www.merriam-webster.com/dictionary/postmodern.

2. "Postmodernism," Public Broadcasting System, accessed May 13, 2020. https://www.pbs.org/faithandreason/gengloss/postm-body.html.

3. "Postmodernism," Modern Museum of Art, accessed May 13, 2020. https://www.moma.org/collection/terms/84.

4. McNeal, *The Present Future*, 8.

5. Pope Francis, *Happiness in This Life: A Passionate Meditation on Earthly Existence*, trans. Oonagh Stransky (New York: Penguin Random House, 2017), 73.

6. King, *Strength to Love*, 14.

7. King, *Strength to Love*, 53.

8. Jamie Ducharme, "Here's How Popular Yoga and Meditation Really Are," Time.com, November 8, 2018, https://time.com/5447850/yoga-meditation-more-popular/.

9. Barna Group, "Americans Feel Good About Counseling," Barna.com, February 27, 2018, https://www.barna.com/research/americans-feel-good-counseling/.

10. Grace Tatter, "Making Time For Mindfulness," Harvard Graduate School of Education, website, January 23, 2019, https://www.gse.harvard.edu/news/uk/19/01/making-time-mindfulness.
11. David Kinnaman, *You Lost Me: Why Young Christians Are Leaving Church* (Grand Rapids, MI: Baker Books, 2011), 172.
12. Pope Francis, *Happiness in This Life*, 14.
13. Pope Francis, *Happiness in This Life*, 20.

5. Time and Understanding ·

1. "Selah," *Merriam-Webster.com Dictionary*, accessed May 14, 2020, https://www.merriam-webster.com/dictionary/selah.
2. Richard Rohr, "Interspiritual Mysticism," CAC.org, August 9, 2019, https://cac.org/listening-for-the-genuine-2019-08-09/.
3. King, *Strength to Love*, 131.
4. King, *Strength to Love*, 75.
5. Peter Enns, *The Bible and the Believer* (New York: Oxford University Press, 2012), 160.

6. Bigger

1. Ilia Delio, "Grounding God in Evolution," *The Bible for Normal People*, podcast, episode 134, 33:00, July 27, 2020, https://peteenns.com/interview-with-ilia-delio-grounding-god-in-evolution/.
2. Wil Gafney, "Womanist Midrash," *The Bible for Normal People*, podcast, episode 46, 13:00.
3. Richard Rohr, "Faith Teaches," CAC.org, July 23, 2019, https://cac.org/faith-teaches-2019-07-23/.
4. Jared Byas, "Do We Know God Is Good From the Bible?" *The Bible for Normal People*, podcast, episode 94, 24:00, July 28, 2019, https://peteenns.com/do-we-know-god-is-good-from-the-bible/.
5. Pew Research Center, *"When Americans Say They Believe in God, What Do They Mean?"*
6. "Institution," *Merriam-Webster.com Dictionary*, accessed November, 2, 2020, https://www.merriam-webster.com/dictionary/institution.
7. King, *Strength to Love*, 25.
8. King, *Strength to Love*, 26.
9. Brad Jersak, "The Bible and Orthodox Faith," *The Bible for Normal People*, podcast, episode 71, 7:00, December 9, 2018, https://peteenns.com/the-bible-and-orthodox-faith/.
10. "Ecumenical Councils," EpiscopalChurch.org, accessed May 17, 2020, https://episcopalchurch.org/library/glossary/ecumenical-councils.

11. Karl Keating, "The 21 Ecumenical Councils," Catholic Answers, website, June 1, 1993, accessed May 17, 2020, https://www.catholic.com/magazine/print-edition/the-21-ecumenical-councils.

12. Richard Rohr, "Simply Living the Gospel," CAC.org, February 2, 2020, https://cac.org/simply-living-the-gospel-2020-02-02/.

13. "Religion," *Merriam-Webster.com Dictionary*, accessed May 16, 2020, https://www.merriam-webster.com/dictionary/religion.

14. Richard Rohr, "The Practice of Awe and Wonder," *Another Name for Every Thing with Richard Rohr*, podcast, 1:01:00, April 25, 2020, https://cac.org/podcasts/the-practice-of-awe-and-wonder/.

7. Everywhere, Everything

1. Pew Research Center, *"When Americans Say They Believe in God, What Do They Mean?"*

2. Pew Research Center, *"When Americans Say They Believe in God, What Do They Mean?"*

3. Carl Jung, *Four Archetypes*, trans. R.F.C. Hull (Princeton, NJ: Princeton University Press, 2010), 92.

4. Søren Kierkegaard quoted in Keller, *The Reason for God*, 162.

5. Pope Francis, *Happiness in This Life*, 3.

6. Rob Bell, *Velvet Elvis: Repainting the Christian Faith* (Grand Rapids, MI: Zondervan, 2005), 91.

7. Brad Jersak, "The Bible and Orthodox Faith," *The Bible for Normal People*, podcast, episode 71, 22:00.

8. Christian Reformed Church, *What It Means to Be Reformed: An Identity Statement*, CRCNA.org, 2016, 42, https://www.crcna.org/sites/default/files/what_it_means_-to_be_reformed.pdf.

8. Now

1. Antonia Blumberg, "American Religion Has Never Looked Quite Like It Does Today," Huffington Post, website, April 15, 2016, https://www.huffpost.com/entry/american-religion-trends_n_570c21cee4b0836057a235ad.

2. Paul Mills et al., "Change in Sense of Nondual Awareness and Spiritual Awakening in Response to a Multidimensional Well-Being Program," *The Journal of Alternative and Complementary Science* 00, no. 00 (2017): 5, DOI: 10.1089/acm.2017.0160.

3. Douglas Yeung and Margret T. Martin, "Spiritual Fitness and Resilience: A Review of Constructs, Measures, and Links to Well-Being," RAND.org, 2013, 39, https://www.rand.org/pubs/research_reports/RR100.html.

4. Sheila Patel et al., "Psychosocial Effects of a Holistic Ayurvedic Approach to Well-Being in Health and Wellness Courses," *Global Advances in Health and Medicine* 8 (2019): 9, DOI: 10.1177/2164956119843814.

5. Fahri Karakas, "Spirituality and Performance in Organizations," *Journal of Business Ethics* 94, no. 1 (June 2010): 89, https://www.jstor.org/stable/40665201.

6. Bell, *Velvet Elvis,* 21.

7. McLaren, *The Secret Message of Jesus,* 36.

8. McLaren, *The Secret Message of Jesus,* 37.

9. Bart D. Ehrman, *Heaven and Hell,* NY: Simon & Schuster, 2020, 83.

10. Peter Enns, "Pete and Jared Talk about the Afterlife," *The Bible for Normal People,* podcast, episode 121, 4:00 and 34:00, March 29, 2020, https://peteenns.com/episode-121-the-afterlife/.

11. Jared Byas, "Pete and Jared Talk about the Afterlife," *The Bible for Normal People,* podcast, episode 121, 3:00 and 34:00.

12. Peter Enns, "Pete and Jared Talk about the Afterlife," *The Bible for Normal People,* podcast, episode 121, 4:00 and 11:00.

13. Ehrman, xix.

14. Ehrman, 86.

15. Meghan Henning, "Does Hell Exist?" *The Bible for Normal People,* podcast, episode 118, 28:00, March 8, 2020. https://peteenns.com/meghan-henning-does-hell-exist/.

16. Meghan Henning, "Does Hell Exist?" *The Bible for Normal People,* podcast, episode 118, 29:00.

17. Richard Rohr, "Hell, The Devil and the Afterlife," *Another Name for Every Thing with Richard Rohr,* podcast, episode 3, 22:00, August 17, 2019, https://cac.org/podcasts/3-hell-the-devil-and-the-afterlife/.

18. Richard Rohr, "Hell, The Devil and the Afterlife," *Another Name for Every Thing with Richard Rohr,* podcast, episode 3, 19:00.

19. Richard Rohr, "Hell, The Devil and the Afterlife," *Another Name for Every Thing with Richard Rohr,* podcast, episode 3, 17:00.

20. Brian McLaren, *Finding Our Way Again: The Return of the Ancient Practices* (Nashville: Thomas Nelson, 2008), 69.

21. Richard Rohr, "Hell, The Devil and the Afterlife," *Another Name for Every Thing with Richard Rohr,* podcast, episode 3, 22:00.

9. The Way

1. Barna Group, "Signs of Decline & Hope Among Metrics in Faith."

2. Carl Jung quoted in Richard Rohr, *Falling Upward: A Spirituality for the Two Halves of Life* (San Francisco: Jossey-Bass, 2011), 1.

3. Richard Rohr, "Goal – Alternative Orthodoxy (Theme 7)," *Another Name for Every Thing with Richard Rohr,* podcast, 19:00, July, 18, 2020, https://cac.org/podcasts/goal-alternative-orthodoxy-theme-7/.

4. Philip Yancey, *What's So Amazing About Grace?* (Grand Rapids: Zondervan, 1997), 13.

5. Richard Rohr, "Goal – Alternative Orthodoxy (Theme 7)," *Another Name for Every Thing with Richard Rohr,* podcast, 18:00.

10. The Symbol

1. Yomi Kazeem, "By 2060, Six of the World's 10 Largest Countries Will Be in Africa," WeForum.org, April 10, 2019, https://www.weforum.org/agenda/2019/04/africa-is-set-to-be-the-global-center-of-christianity-for-the-next-50-years/.
2. Bell, *Velvet Elvis*, 139.
3. Sylvia Keesmaat and Brian Walsh, "Resisting Empire in the Book of Romans," *The Bible for Normal People,* podcast, episode 93, 13:00, July 14, 2019, https://peteenns.com/resisting-empire-in-the-book-of-romans/.
4. Bell, *Velvet Elvis*, 134.

11. Truth

1. St. Thomas Aquinas quoted in Richard Rohr, "Simply Living the Gospel."
2. Richard Rohr, "Introduction to Christian Mysticism," CAC.org, July 17, 2019, https://cac.org/our-response-2019-07-17/.
3. Pete Rollins, "The Last Guru with Pete Rollins," *The RobCast,* podcast, episode 255, 21:00, October 6, 2019.
4. Pete Rollins, "The Last Guru with Pete Rollins," *The RobCast,* podcast, episode 255, 29:00.
5. Deepak Chopra, "Why the Greatest Mystery Is You," The Chopra Foundation, website, May 13, 2019, https://www.choprafoundation.org/consciousness/why-the-greatest-mystery-is-you/.
6. King, *Strength to Love*, 13.
7. King, *Strength to Love*, 14.
8. Keller, *The Reason for God*, 4.

12. Questions

1. McLaren, *The Secret Message of Jesus,* 39.
2. Rob Bell, "You Have Come to This Mountain," *The RobCast*, podcast, 13:00, May 18, 2020, https://robbell.podbean.com/e/you-have-come-to-this-mountain/.
3. McNeal, *The Present Future*, 34.
4. Kinnaman and Lyons, *unChristian*, 33.

14. Maturity

1. Pew Research Center, "America's Changing Religious Landscape."
2. Richard Rohr, "The Container and the Contents," CAC.org, March 18, 2019, https://cac.org/the-container-and-the-contents-2019-03-18/.

3. Peter Enns, "How the Bible Actually Works," *The Bible for Normal People,* podcast, episode 112, 21:00, December 15, 2019, https://thebiblefornormalpeople.podbean.com/e/episode-112-pete-and-jared-how-how-the-bible-actually-works-works/.

4. McNeal, *The Present Future,* 143.

5. McLaren, *The Secret Message of Jesus,* 97.

6. Kent R. Hunter, *Restoring Civility: Lessons from the Master: Your Path to Rediscover Respect* (Corunna, IN: Church Doctor Publishing, 2020), xi.

7. Eugene Peterson, foreword to *The Leadership Ellipse: Shaping How We Lead by Who We Are,* by Robert A. Fryling (Downer's Grove, IL: Intervarsity Press, 2010), x.

8. Wil Gafney, "Womanist Midrash," *The Bible for Normal People,* podcast, episode 105, 4:00, October 27, 2019, https://thebiblefornormalpeople.podbean.com/e/episode-46-wil-gafney-womanist-midrash/.

9. Wil Gafney, "Womanist Midrash," *The Bible for Normal People,* podcast, episode 105, 26:00.

10. Miguel De La Torre, "Diverse Voices in Biblical Scholarship," *The Bible for Normal People,* podcast, episode 127, 17:00, May 10, 2020, https://thebiblefornormalpeople.podbean.com/e/episode-127-miguel-de-la-torre-diverse-voices-in-biblical-scholarship/.

11. Miguel De La Torre, "Diverse Voices in Biblical Scholarship," *The Bible for Normal People,* podcast, episode 127, 17:00.

12. Pope Francis, *Happiness in This Life,* 14.

13. Pete Rollins, "The Last Guru with Pete Rollins," *The RobCast,* podcast, episode 255, 33:00.

14. Pope Francis, *Happiness in This Life,* 28.

15. Practice

1. King, *Strength to Love,* p 40.

2. "Global Weight Management Market 2019–2024: Breakdown by Diet, Equipment, Service, and Region — ReseachAndMarkets.com," BusinessWire.com, August 26, 2019, accessed June 5, 2020, https://www.businesswire.com/news/home/20190826005243/en/Global-Weight-Management-Market-2019-2024-Breakdown-Diet.

3. Richard Rohr, "Simply Living the Gospel," CAC.org, February 2, 2020.

16. Connection and Community

1. Jean Vanier, *Becoming Human* (Mahwah, NJ: Paulist Press, 1998), 33.

2. Keller, *The Reason for God,* xix.

3. Thom S. Rainer, "Hope for Dying Churches," FactsandTrends.com, January 16, 2018, https://factsandtrends.net/2018/01/16/hope-for-dying-churches/.

4. Taylor Billings Russell, "The Conundrum of Counting Churches," Center for Analytics, Research and Data - United Church of Christ, website, July 22, 2019, https://carducc.wordpress.com/2019/07/22/the-conundrum-of-counting-churches/.

5. "The Sunday slump: the virus is decelerating church in America," The Economist, website, May 23, 2020, https://www.economist.com/united-states/2020/05/23/the-virus-is-accelerating-dechurching-in-america.

6. McNeal, *The Present Future*, 34.

17. More

1. King, *Strength to Love*, 131.

2. Jersak, "The Bible and Orthodox Faith," *The Bible for Normal People,* podcast, episode 71, 13:00.

3. Matthias Henze, "The Bible and Second Temple Judaism," *The Bible for Normal People,* podcast, episode 128, 36:00, May 17, 2020, https://peteenns.com/matthias-henze-the-bible-second-temple-judaism/.

4. Peter Enns, "The Bible and Second Temple Judaism," *The Bible for Normal People*, podcast, episode 128, 37:00.

ABOUT THE AUTHOR

Jeff Widenhofer graduated from the US Naval Academy and was commissioned as an ensign in 1997. He then served nine years as a Navy officer, completing three deployments to the Middle East as a helicopter pilot, followed by a tour as an associate professor at the US Merchant Marine Academy in Kings Point, New York. After the Navy he transitioned to a career as a professional guitarist in New York City. He has performed in both the most obscure and the most prestigious venues in the music industry—clubs, theaters, studios, churches, as well as Broadway shows and national television productions. In 2014 he was in contention for two Oscar nominations for his music in the film *MURPH: The Protector*. He holds a bachelor's degree in history from the US Naval Academy, a master's degree in music from the University of Colorado, and is currently pursuing a master's degree in social work at the University of Denver. He lives with his wife and two daughters in Boulder, Colorado.

CPSIA information can be obtained
at www.ICGtesting.com
Printed in the USA
BVHW031802120821
614283BV00002B/340